Evaluating Complex Business Reports:

A Guide for Executives

Evaluating Complex Business Reports:

A Guide for Executives

Eli P. Cox III

DOW JONES-IRWIN
Homewood, Illinois 60430

ISBN 0-87094-431-2

Library of Congress Catalog Card No. 83–73363

Printed in the United States of America

1 2 3 4 5 6 7 8 9 0 K 1 0 9 8 7 6 5 4

PREFACE

This book is written for those business managers who must base major decisions on the information gathered by others through research. The book attempts to provide an understanding of the essential qualities of business research so that managers can see through the technical detail of a research project and assess its basic strengths and weaknesses. At the least, managers should be able to ask researchers enough intelligent questions to ensure that the information foundation they are basing their decisions on is a sound one. While no understanding of the technical aspects of research is assumed, it is expected that the reader has prior experience with research applications.

Scientific research is nothing more than a relatively efficient and highly formal way of learning from experience. It promises significant advances in business practice when the insight and wisdom of managers are effectively teamed with the tools and techniques of the scientific researcher. Unfortunately, managers and researchers tend to speak different languages and have different views of the world. This book is dedicated to breaking down the barriers to communication between the two groups. Researchers will remain underutilized and mistrusted, and managers will keep making the same mistakes until these barriers are breached.

This guide for evaluating research projects has developed over a number of years as managers and MBA students have taught me while I have tried to share with them my appreciation for the potential benefits of good research. Scores of individuals have used earlier drafts of this book to critique research in a wide variety of areas. I wish to thank them for their help and hope that this book represents a small repayment.

It is hoped that the reader will gain some pleasure and insight when first reading through the book and will find it useful thereafter as a desk reference.

I also wish to thank my sister, Ruth Anne Payne of Temple, Barker and Sloane, for her comments and suggestions. My colleague Rohit Deshpande has also been most helpful and constructive in his comments. Finally, a word of thanks to my wife, Ardis, who has once again demonstrated that one of the highest forms of love is the willingness to proofread.

Eli P. Cox III

CONTENTS

CHAPTER 1

Judging the Quality of Research-Based Information

Research is an organized method of finding out what you are going to do when you can't keep on doing what you are doing now.

Charles F. Kettering

I always find that statistics are hard to swallow and impossible to digest. The only one I can ever remember is that if all of the people who go to sleep in church were laid end to end they would be a lot more comfortable.

Mrs. Robert A. Taft

This book is a nontechnical guide for managers to use in evaluating the research reports they depend on when making important business decisions.

Even in a friendly game of poker, the winner shows his cards. We expect our best friend to show us the straight that he announces has just beaten our three aces. Likewise, it is a good idea for managers to see the researchers' hands, for they may find that they are getting more or less than they had bargained for. This is critical because the game is not always friendly and the stakes are almost always high.

While most managers recognize the importance of research, they have little interest in research per se. They are interested in the information produced by research and not the process of producing it. Furthermore, many feel that they do not have the training, experience, or even the time necessary to evaluate such technical work.

This first chapter discusses the importance of judging the quality of research-based information. Its first section illustrates the way in which an apparently minor change in research procedures can produce a major change in results. The second section presents the example of an executive who used an earlier draft of this book to uncover major problems found in a poor research project. The final sections provide a more detailed statement of the objectives of the book and a description of its organization.

• GARBAGE IN—GARBAGE OUT

Most managers realize that making important corporate decisions with inadequate information is equivalent to NASA sending up a multimillion-dollar rocket with little or nothing invested in the guidance system. However, it is not enough that managers appreciate, and thus acquire, information on which to base their decisions. They must also be able to appraise the quality of the data that have been gathered for their use. They should not place themselves in a position of being forced to accept the reported results of research at face value.

To emphasize this point, consider the surveys in Tables 1.1 and 1.2. Both present results using the same "press release" format, but they contain contradictory findings. In the first survey, 61 percent of the respondents support trade protection, while only 18 percent support it in the second survey. The reader is incapable of determining which, if either, of the surveys is valid without knowing how they were conducted.

Table 1.1 presents the results of a survey which utilized a question originally employed in a survey by the *New York Times* and CBS:

> Which do you think is more important—to protect workers' jobs at the cost of higher prices for some products, or to be able to buy foreign goods at lower prices at the cost of some unemployment in this country?

TABLE 1.1

Texas Trade Protection Survey

Residents of Austin, Texas, hold attitudes which are strongly in favor of trade protection for American industries, a recent survey reveals. A random sample of 240 households was interviewed by telephone. The results, which are accurate to within plus or minus 6 percentage points, are:

Position on Trade Protection	Responses	
	Number	*Percent*
For	146	60.8
Against	94	39.2
Total	240	100.0

An editorial in *The Wall Street Journal* (June 30, 1983) shared the lamentations of the spokesman for the White House Office of the Special Representative for Trade Negotiations, who suggested that the pro-protection result of the original survey was an artifact of the question's wording. The editorial presented an alternative formulation of the question which would likely produce the opposite result:

> Which would you prefer—effective price competition associated with some unemployment in noncompetitive industries, or federal interference with competition that would

TABLE 1.2

Texas Trade Protection Survey

Residents of Austin, Texas, hold highly critical attitudes toward trade protection for American industries, a recent survey reveals. A random sample of 240 households was interviewed by telephone. The results, which are accurate to within plus or minus 5 percentage points, are:

Position on Trade Protection	Responses	
	Number	*Percent*
For	42	17.5
Against	198	82.5
Total	240	100.0

result in higher prices and a higher level of unemployment in the American work force as a whole?

The two sets of results presented in the figures were obtained from a small experiment I conducted to determine the impact this difference in question wording might have on the answers given by individuals in a telephone interview. The two versions of the question were included on separate forms of a questionnaire which were placed alternately in a stack and used in interviews of 480 respondents. Accordingly, the only factor that can account for the large difference in survey results is the wording of the question.

Actually, neither of the surveys was valid because the questions tend to editorialize as well as ask. On the one hand, no one wants to make a personal contribution to the nation's unemployment rate. On the other hand, federal interference is not in vogue these days. Both questions fail because they provide only one side of a complex, two-sided economic issue.

Certainly, few research reports are designed to produce biased results. However, *the way in which a project is conducted dictates the nature of the results in every case.*

• *CAVEAT LECTOR*

Caveat lector, or reader beware, is an appropriate warning for managers who must depend upon others for vital information. This is the case even when the best of research talent is at the managers' disposal and funds are not significantly limited. The research conducted by a highly competent corporate staff may be limited in scope, thus leading to the danger that the managers may unknowingly make a decision beyond the limits of support by the project. The most eminent research and consulting firms may have their work undermined by their lack of knowledge concerning the particular industry or product they are examining. The only available research may have been conducted by a third party who has a stake in the outcome of the decision, and thus the research must be suspect. Finally, statistics published by government and private organizations are usually based on research methods with limitations the manager should be aware of.

This need to look under the surface of an attractive report or presentation is dramatically illustrated by the experience of a businessman who used an earlier draft of this book. The businessman is the general counsel of a small manufacturing company, which is a subsidiary of one of the Fortune 500 firms. Corporate management commissioned one of the top five consulting firms in the country to conduct a study to assess the market potential of a piece of industrial equipment manufactured by the subsidiary costing between $300,000 and $500,000.

The results of this $50,000 survey were revealed in a presentation made at the subsidiary's headquarters. The findings indicated that the market potential for the machine was quite limited and did not justify the considerable investment being requested by the management of the subsidiary. The counsel was not normally involved in such matters but happened to attend the presentation. Great disappointment about the study's results was expressed after the meeting, and the counsel indicated that he had some real questions about the conclusions. As he did not have any background in research, he obtained a draft of this book and proceeded to evaluate the report.

He asked the marketing manager for a copy of the research report, but was given only photocopies of the transparencies used in the presentation. The materials did not include a copy of the questionnaire used and contained virtually no details concerning how the study was conducted. Also, no comprehensive presentation was made of the data analysis, as only selected statistics were presented to support the conclusions of the report.

The counsel inquired at both the local and corporate levels and found that no detailed research report had been provided by the consultants. After contacting the

consultants who had handled the contract, he was finally given a description of the research methodology
and a copy of each of the completed questionnaires.

As less than a hundred two-page questionnaires were
involved, the counsel took a couple of hours and analyzed the data by hand. What he found was most revealing:

1. There were minor discrepancies between the statistics found in the report and his own calculations.
This suggested errors on someone's part or that the consultants' unstated procedures (e.g., how to treat unan-
swered questions) were different from his own.

2. He found that the consultants had obtained a list
of the company's existing customers from the service
department and had sent the questionnaire to them. This
was problematic in that the contact person for service
problems in a company may not be the appropriate person to interview regarding the purchase of additional
machines. As well, the use of this list meant that the
study excluded all potential customers who had not yet
purchased the machine. This omission was of particular
importance since the type of machine was radically different from other machines and had only been on the
market for a short time.

3. In examining the questionnaire, he found a dubi-
ous sequence of questions. The first question asked the
respondent to indicate the likelihood that his company
would purchase one of the machines in the near future.
The second asked which, if any, of the six options listed
would likely be purchased. The third asked how much
the company would be willing to pay for the machine.
The report discussed the answer to the third question
as if it asked only about the price of the basic machine
without any of the options. In contrast, the counsel felt
that since the preceding question asked about options,
the respondent might have been led to believe that the
machine mentioned in the price question included the
options that had been selected by the respondent previ-
ously.

4. The counsel found that all of the respondents were treated similarly in the analysis. In examining their job titles, it was found that they ranged from a vice president of engineering who had signature authority for hundreds of thousands of dollars to another respondent who indicated that he was simply an engineer who had been on his first job for a few weeks. The counsel sorted the questionnaires into a pile for those who would likely be able to buy the machine, or at least have a major influence on the purchase process, and another for those obviously of little influence. Not surprisingly, he found that those who seemed not to be in a position to make such a purchase decision indicated that they would not be likely to purchase the machine.

In contrast, those whose positions suggested that they would be in a position to make such a purchase decision indicated that they were likely to buy the machine. By projecting the results from this group to other companies in the sample and making modest assumptions concerning potential customers, the counsel was able to draw the exact opposite conclusion concerning the market potential for the machine.

When the president of the subsidiary saw the results of the counsel's evaluation of the study, he became irate and called the corporate chairman and CEO who called a meeting of all interested parties. The consultants concluded the meeting by saying that they would look into the matter. It is interesting to speculate about what would have happened if the counsel had not conducted his investigation.

One may argue that this example is unusual and that the job of decision making is sufficiently taxing that it is ultimately necessary to depend upon the internal research staff or hired consultants to gather quality information. This is certainly true. However, there are several reasons why managers should evaluate the quality of a proposed research project as well as the quality of research-based information once it has been gathered.

First, *the answers provided by the researchers can
never transcend the limitations of the research questions provided by the managers.* If the researchers are
left to their own devices during the design stage of a
study, there is little guarantee that they will anticipate
all of the information requirements of the managers.

Second, *every research project has its limitations,
and there is always a danger that the conclusions of
the research cannot be extended to the actual problem
at hand.* For example, a research project evaluating pro-
duction engineers' assessments of competitive pieces of
machinery may be limited to the extent that the engineers are not solely responsible for the purchase decision.

The third reason why a manager should be able to
evaluate research is that *projects done by even the best
researchers may have errors.* In contrast to research
limitations, research errors are problems which, if identified, can be addressed without increasing the costs of
the project. Research errors can be more severe than
research limitations in that they are more likely to produce false and misleading information in research projects. The trade protection surveys presented earlier illustrate this point.

A fourth reason is that managers often have to depend on research gathered by others. Thus, *managers
may not have any control over the quality of the researchers or of the research they produce, but their decisions depend upon that quality.*

A final reason is that *managers may be given research information produced by others that has been
biased intentionally.*

• OBJECTIVE OF THE BOOK

If it is accepted that managers should be able to evaluate
research, then the question remains: Can managers with
little technical training and experience in research evaluate the work of others who have that training and experience? The answer to this question is *yes.* Managers

can combine a general understanding of the potential pitfalls of research with their own experience and common sense to evaluate the quality of research-based information and to be able to ask the researchers intelligent questions and probe areas of possible weakness in their work.

As the scope and complexity of business decisions increase, managers must be particularly confident in the quality of the information they depend on. This book has been written to enable managers to evaluate technical research reports. It assumes that while most managers are quite familiar with the application of research in their particular area, they may not have the background and training to conduct the research and thus are apprehensive about evaluating it technically. This book should serve as a nontechnical guide in making this sort of evaluation.

A draft of the book has been used for more than five years as a guide for evaluating research projects. The projects have been quite diverse but have fallen into three categories. The first type of study has involved surveys designed to acquire a better *understanding of the decision-making environment,* such as:

- A municipality's survey of its employees prior to entering negotiations with an insurance company on a fringe benefits package.
- Research estimating the market potential for a new consumer product.
- A survey assessing the position of members of a trade association during the development of a legislative program.

Examples of the second type of study concern *tests of decision alternatives* facing managers:

- An evaluation of a new weapon in a battle simulation.
- A test by a motel chain of the cost-effectiveness of four control devices designed to increase the energy efficiency of room air conditioners.

- A review of the criteria used by a bank in granting loans to small businesses.

The third type of study utilizes *published statistics* in supporting decisions, such as for:

- An application for a charter for a savings and loan based upon demonstration of need in the area.
- A feasibility study for a new hotel.
- A demand forecast for an industrial product.

• ORGANIZATION OF THE BOOK

The remainder of the book consists of five chapters, each covering a special category of problems frequently encountered while conducting business research. Chapter 2 discusses the necessity and, at times, difficulty of researching the right problem. Just as there is the danger that a physician may misdiagnose an illness and prescribe the wrong treatment, so a researcher runs the risk of improperly identifying the problem and conducting irrelevant research.

Chapter 3 deals with the importance of obtaining accurate research measures. Problems encountered in both the design and use of measurement instruments are covered.

Chapter 4 reviews frame error, nonresponse error, selection error, and sampling error as four problems which limit the ability of researchers to apply sample-based results to the larger population from which the sample was selected.

Even if results of a research project are relevant, technically accurate, and can be used to describe the full population, they may not be able to support the conclusions that are implied or that the managers may wish to draw. The focus of the discussion in Chapter 5 is the difficulty of identifying causal relationships through research.

Chapter 6 covers problems which may be found in reporting research results. It discusses what should be looked for in evaluating a research project. Special attention is paid to the use of misleading visual aids. The chapter concludes with a list of questions a manager may use in looking for the research problems discussed throughout this book.

For readers who wish to learn more about the various aspects of the research process, an annotated bibliography is included. It contains the references used for this book as well as other sources of information about business research which may be useful and informative.

CHAPTER 2

Researching the
Right Problem

There is nothing more frightful than ignorance in action.

Goethe

Basic research is what I'm doing when I don't know what I'm doing.

W. H. Auden and L. Kronenberger

On October 25, 1964 Jim Marshall of the Vikings picked up a San Francisco fumble, ran the ball for 66 yards and threw the ball out of the end zone. Unfortunately, the heroic run was in the wrong direction and resulted in a safety. Moral: *Even the most brilliant effort can be harmful if it is misdirected.* This is certainly true when a research project has been initiated before the research problem has been accurately and adequately defined. This chapter discusses the importance and the difficulty of defining business problems prior to conducting research.

When we think of errors in research we normally think of errors of commission, such as when a poor sample has been drawn or questions have been improperly worded. However, errors of omission can be at least as significant as such errors of commission in research projects. The most severe of these involve the failure to research the right problem.

A national brewery, worried about its declining market share on the West Coast, hired a marketing research firm to conduct taste tests in the area. The results of the study revealed that most respondents could not distinguish one beer from another and that the respondents did not feel that the beer in question was significantly better or worse than its competitors.

Unfortunately, the brewery had spent considerable time and money on the research, but it was no closer to the solution. Later it was determined that the problem was in a distribution system that was weak relative to those of competitors, so the question of the technical accuracy of the taste tests was a moot point.

• IDENTIFICATION OF THE PROBLEM

It may seem hardly worth saying that if a research project is to garner information that is useful in helping to make a decision, then the project should be relevant to the problem. In practice, identifying the problem is often the most illusive research task. The symptoms reflecting the problem are generally obvious but the underlying cause may be quite difficult to identify.

Increased employee turnover, for example, may reflect poor working conditions, dissatisfaction with the pay, increased opportunities offered by competitors or a number of other things. If an employee survey is predicated on the assumption that the problem is with working conditions when it is actually due to the existence of higher-paying jobs offered by competitors, then the survey may point to a minor irritant—parking for example—which only serves to distract management's attention from the central problem.

Qualitative versus Quantitative Research

When management and the researchers are not certain as to the nature of the problem, then effective research generally takes place in two phases. The first phase is often referred to as *qualitative research,* and the second is referred to as *quantitative research.*

The qualitative phase is for the purpose of defining the problem. Researchers must play a role which is more akin to that of a detective than what is conventionally viewed to be the role of a researcher. They must work closely with managers to identify the problem and its parameters. The information gathered may be vague, incomplete, and contradictory. Great insight, experience, and tact are required to complete this phase of the research successfully. The results of this phase are the assumptions upon which the final research project rests. Sophisticated researchers recognize that the assumptions may not be correct and thus view them as working hypotheses to be evaluated in the second phase of the research.

The second, quantitative, phase of research assumes that the problem has been adequately defined and attempts to confirm the working hypotheses and make precise estimates of the parameters being studied.

As an example, researchers may be asked to determine why turnover is so high among the employees of a hospital. In the qualitative phase, researchers may hold discussions with hospital administrators and conduct informal interviews with some of its workers to determine why turnover is high. This investigation might indicate that the problem is due to higher-paying jobs with competitors rather than any real dissatisfaction with working conditions. In the second phase, the researchers might employ trained interviewers to conduct formal interviews with a representatively selected sample of employees. Its purpose would be to confirm the problem, identify what percentage of the workers in various job classifications feel that there are better-paying jobs with competitive hospitals, and obtain evidence as to the cost-effectiveness of alternative solutions. In this phase, the researchers depend more on technical skill and training than on intuition. While managers share equal responsibility with researchers for errors in the first phase of the research, responsibility for the second phase rests primarily on the researchers' shoulders, given time and financial constraints imposed by management.

There are two problems frequently encountered in

the qualitative phase of research. The first occurs when management and the researchers are so confident as to the nature and parameters of the problem that the exploratory research stage is treated cursorily or skipped altogether. Such a decision may be appropriate where the quantitative study is simply one in a series being conducted in an environment that is not changing a great deal. However, if there is so much understanding of the research environment that the qualitative phase of a one-shot study can be eliminated, then there should be a real question as to the cost-effectiveness of the quantitative phase as well. More often, managers run a risk of wasting time and money on misdirected quantitative research because the problem was not properly defined through qualitative research.

A second danger is that managers and researchers have so much confidence in the contributions of qualitative research that they do not feel the need to seek confirmation through quantitative research. This used to be common prior to the development of quantitative techniques, but it has increased in frequency with the increased popularity of *focus groups.*

A focus group is simply an unstructured or depth interview conducted with several individuals simultaneously. Often six or eight respondents are invited to a special research facility where they are seated around a conference table or in what appears to be a family living room. The interviewer serves much as a moderator in generating and directing group discussion concerning the research topic.

The popularity of focus group interviews is probably due more to their flashiness in great contrast to the rather drab nature of most other research techniques. Although focus groups are excellent in delineating a research problem, the information they provide may well be highly unreliable.

The potential advantage of focus group interviews versus those conducted individually is that group interaction may generate information which otherwise would not have been discovered, such as points of agreement and disagreement among different types of respondents. However, their popularity is at least partially due to the opportunity for audience involvement, where the audience consists of members of management. For example, most product managers for consumer products sell to millions of consumers through thousands of resellers and thus have little if any direct contact with consumers, except themselves and others in their own homes. Thus, to be able to observe through a two-way mirror a group of consumers discussing a product can be most revealing and even exciting.

While the reaction of managers to focus groups is understandable and great insights can be obtained from them, this does not mean that other, drier forms of research have been successfully replaced. Focus groups are notoriously unreliable. Even if several groups have been interviewed, there is a great danger in attempting to draw definitive conclusions. The problems of an inadequate sample when 75 respondents have participated in focus groups are no less severe than would be experienced if researchers attempted to conduct a national public opinion poll with 75 respondents selected without the benefit of random sampling.

In addition, there is the danger that the interviewer or one of the respondents may lead the group and distort the true opinions of its members. For these reasons, the fact that almost all of the participants in a focus group have positive evaluations of a new product, for example, does not mean that the same can be said about all of its potential customers.

Focus groups can be an invaluable part of the research effort, but they can be dangerous when used by themselves. Qualitative and quantitative research are most effective when used in concert.

• INCLUDING THE RELEVANT VARIABLES

Several years ago I served as an expert witness for a small Texas company that was suing a large Midwestern company which had sold it two franchise outlets of a fast-food Mexican restaurant. The franchises failed despite the fact that the franchisor claimed to have re-search results that were "nationally projectable demon-strating the restaurant's potential for success." The research had been referred to in sales presentations and promotional materials but had not actually been shown to the franchisees. During the discovery process of the lawsuit, it was found that the research was voluminous, expensive, and had been done by firms of national repu-tation.

Unfortunately, although the research was techni-cally accurate, it did not address one of the issues critical to the success of the restaurant in the marketplace. The research failed to take into account the way in which consumers' evaluations of the franchise varied with their degree of familiarity with Mexican food. Those who were unfamiliar with Mexican food tended to like the franchise's fare, while those who were familiar with Mexican food generally did not like it. Most of the re-search was conducted in the Midwest, where consumers were generally unfamiliar with Mexican food. It turned out that the franchise originated in a city where less than 1 percent of the population was Spanish speaking, while half of the population was Spanish speaking in the area in Texas where the franchises were opened. A lemon-flavored fried pie called a lemonito was pre-sented as Mexican fare in the franchisor's research, but it certainly would not be accepted in a region where the majority of households prepare some Mexican food at home.

While preparing for the trial, I ran across a newspa-per article relating the story of a man whose leg was amputated because of poor circulation due to diabetes. The operation was technically a great success, but unfor-tunately the surgeons had removed the wrong leg. They graciously agreed to perform the second operation free of charge. I felt that the research I had reviewed was similar to the surgery in that it was acceptable from a technical point of view—the findings were correct as far as they went. *The research failed because it missed the point.*

In another situation, a manufacturer developed a

dispenser for shampoo and liquid soap which was to be cemented to the side of the shower stall. Management was confident in the product's potential for success because of the favorable consumer reaction, especially among young adults, as indicated by extensive marketing research. The product was introduced with disappointing results. Later analysis found that many of the young adults who liked the product in principle lived in apartments and were concerned about losing their rental deposits if they installed anything permanently in the showers.

As these two examples illustrate, a pitfall similar to the failure to define the problem correctly is the failure to include all relevant variables. Research has only done half a job when it has properly identified the problem confronting management; it must define the problem broadly enough to provide direction in decision making to managers. A project which is based on a proper definition of the problem but is not broad enough in scope to suggest a solution or to identify obstacles to the attainment of that solution is not economically justifiable. In the case of the Mexican food franchise, familiarity with the product category was not considered; in the case of the soap dispenser, the research considered the use but not the installation of the product.

• CONCLUSION

Solutions often become obvious when the problem has been clearly and fully defined. Unfortunately, problem definition is often a very difficult matter and may itself be an objective of research. In most cases both qualitative and quantitative research are indispensable in the information-gathering process. Especially in the qualitative phases of research, it is critical that managers share their insights and experience with the researchers. Managers who dismiss researchers and research problems from their minds until the results are in, in order to deal with more important problems, are apt to falsely blame the researchers for wasting time and money.

CHAPTER 3

Ensuring Accurate Measurement

There are two kinds of statistics, the kind you look up and the kind you make up.

Rex Stout

A statistician is a person who draws a mathematically precise line from an unwarranted assumption to a foregone conclusion.

Anonymous

We have to be very careful how we measure things because once measures are in place, they take on a life of their own—no matter how bad they are to begin with. The cost-of-living index was developed to measure inflation, but it has been a cause of inflation because it gives an unrealistically high estimate of the cost of operating a household.

Measuring things in a meaningful way is particularly difficult outside the physical sciences. The difficulties encountered in developing business measures are the focus of this chapter.

Although it is the joint responsibility of managers and researchers to ensure that a research effort involves properly defining the problem and specifying the relevant variables, the responsibility for technical accuracy rests primarily with the researchers. Yet managers need to be aware of the potential for problems of a technical nature so that they are able to assess the quality of research-based information they use.

Technical accuracy concerns both how well individuals or objects are measured and the success with which the measures describing a sample of individuals or objects can be used to describe a larger group. The first of these questions concerns measurement error, which is the topic of this chapter. The problem of generalizing from samples is discussed in the next chapter.

Fundamentally, research involves measuring things. *Measurement error* exists when there is a discrepancy between the *true value* of a measure of an individual or object and the *estimated value* of that measure. Such a discrepancy can exist when a single variable is involved, such as when an estimate is made of a person's income, or when there is a measure based on a composite of a number of variables, as when a manager is trying to estimate a person's potential for employment in a particular job by use of a psychological test. Thus, measurement error exists when the score chosen to represent a single person or object does not successfully reflect the extent to which the person or object possesses the attribute of concern.

To understand measurement error it is important to be able to differentiate among the concepts of measure, measurement, scale, and scaling. A *measure* is a score assigned to a person or object which indicates the extent to which it possesses an attribute. Age, taxable income, IQ, SAT score, and golf handicap are all measures used frequently to represent individuals.

Measurement is the process of assigning a measure to the person or object. The procedures used to administer the SAT to high school students constitute measurement. Auditing is a profession dedicated to the elimination of measurement error in financial reporting.

A *scale* is a measurement instrument used in assigning a score to a person or an object. The scale can be an electronic or mechanical device, such as that used to measure a person's blood pressure; or the scale can be simply a pencil and paper test, as in the case of the SAT.

Scaling is the process of developing the scale or measurement instrument. Scaling is rather straightforward in the physical sciences, but it is extremely complex where humans are involved, as is usually the case in business research. For example, not only do researchers fail to agree as to how intelligence is to be measured, they also disagree about what it is and even whether it exists. As well, the criticism concerning the economic measure of the money supply centers around what money is rather than how it is to be measured.

Measurement error can be encountered either because of problems in the measurement process or because the measurement instrument was not properly designed in the first place. Before these problems are discussed, however, it would be useful to review the criteria used in judging the quality of measures.

• STANDARDS FOR JUDGING THE QUALITY OF MEASURES

There are two basic standards for judging the quality of measures—instrument validity and instrument reliability. In popular usage and in some research reports, these terms have lost virtually all of their meaning and are synonymous with *good.* However, they have technical definitions, and extensive research has been done in the field of psychometrics to develop standards for these qualities of measures. The following discussion will review these qualities in only the most general terms.

Instrument validity refers to the overall success of an instrument in measuring what it is supposed to measure. A person is concerned with the validity of an IQ test when asking whether a set of questions that are culture-bound and education-bound are truly capable of measuring the intellectual ability of those who take it. If those individuals with higher scores generally tend to have a higher level of intelligence than those with low scores, then the test is said to be valid.

The second criterion for evaluating a measurement instrument is *instrument reliability.* Instrument reliability refers to the ability of measures to be consistent over time and across situations. In one respect, an executive placement test is reliable if a person takes it twice and gets the same result each time. It is quite possible, however, that the individual will answer differently on the second administration of the test because of forgetfulness, a different mood, or because of the experience gained from having taken it once already rather than because of increased ability. In another respect, a measure is considered reliable if someone finds two objects weigh the same and they actually have the same true weight. (Bathroom scales are notably unreliable because of their spring mechanisms.)

To gain a better understanding of the distinction between validity and reliability, it might be helpful to consider the measures which might be taken using two different types of rulers. A fisherman's ruler, found in many sporting goods stores, indicates that the objects it measures are 12 inches long when they are actually only 8. It will produce invalid measures (and good fish stories) in that all of the fish measured with it will appear 50 percent longer than they actually are.

In contrast, a rubber ruler exactly 12 inches in length will produce measures which are unreliable to the extent that the ruler expands and contracts with usage and changes in temperature. If a person measured a fish with it 10 times, there might be 10 different measures indicating the scale's unreliability. However, if these 10 different measures were averaged and the amount equalled the true length of the fish, then it could be said that the rubber ruler produced valid but unreliable measures.

Another way of distinguishing between instrument validity and reliability and recognizing that it is possible to have both, neither, or just one is to imagine that measuring things is like hitting a target with a rifle. In Figure 3.1, four marksmen have each fired four shots at the target. By analogy, marksman A's aim is valid and reliable in that the shots are consistently in the center of the target. Marksman B's is invalid but reliable in that the shots are bad, but consistently so. Marksman C's

FIGURE 3.1

Marksmen A, B, C, and D Put Four Shots in a Target

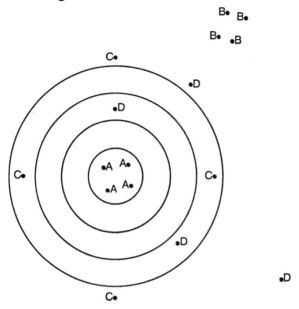

aim is unreliable but valid in that the shots are scattered, but are centered on the bull's-eye. Finally, Marksman D's aim is unreliable and invalid in that the shots are scattered and to the bottom right of the target.

Ideally, measurement produces results which are completely valid and reliable, but this is impossible in practice. Even in the physical sciences, human error introduces some unreliability into what are very accurate measures. In business research, one hopes that the measures used are basically valid and that unreliability has been kept to a sufficiently low level that the scores can be meaningfully interpreted.

Researchers generally prefer to sacrifice some degree of reliability in order to gain validity. This is why standardized intelligence and placement tests are in common usage even though their unreliability is widely recognized. The use of a person's hat size to indicate intelligence would not be subject to the vagaries of cultural and educational differences that plague the standardized tests. In addition, such measures would be easily obtained and thus their stability across individuals and situations would make them highly reliable. However, few now argue that there is any relationship between head size and intelligence, and so it is on the basis of invalidity that these measures are not in common usage.

Terms related to instrument validity and reliability are *accuracy* and *precision.* Accuracy is roughly equivalent to validity and refers to the overall correctness of a research finding. Precision is similar to reliability in that it refers to the exactitude of a research finding. The distinction is important for two reasons. First, it is possible to have either one without the other. Second, we often have a false sense that precise statements are always superior to imprecise ones.

The statement that on August 12, 1983 the British pound traded for $1.4940 is both accurate and precise. The statement that it traded for approximately $1.50 is also accurate but not very precise. In contrast, it is inaccurate but precise to say that it traded for $1.7862 and it would be neither accurate nor precise to say that it traded for $1.80. If one person argues that the true value was approximately $1.50 and another argues that it was exactly $1.7862, there is often a tendency to assume that the latter is a better estimate because precision creates the illusion of knowledge.

In summary, it can be said that validity and reliability are most desirable qualities in measurement instruments and researchers must strive to obtain them. *In practice, business researchers can never eliminate measurement error, but they can reasonably be expected to provide measures which are essentially valid and have a sufficient degree of reliability to differentiate among the individuals or objects being measured.* What this means, for example, is that if researchers are evaluating alternative investments in terms of internal rate of return, a difference between 10 and 20 percent is probably significant but a difference between 10 and 12 is probably not.

• MEASUREMENT ERROR DUE TO AN IMPROPERLY DESIGNED SCALE

As was mentioned earlier, measurement error can occur either because a measurement instrument is improperly designed or because it is improperly used. Ambiguity, wording bias, and specification error will be discussed here as three major problems encountered in designing a measurement instrument.

Ambiguity occurs when there is faulty communication in a personal interview or a written questionnaire. For instance, when an interviewer asks a poorly worded question, the respondent may misinterpret it and answer inaccurately. Additionally, a poorly worded answer may lead to misunderstanding on the part of the interviewer. A question such as "What is your income?" can involve ambiguity in both directions. Respondents may not know whether income includes only wages and salary or additional income earned with a part-time job. A respondent may answer $20,000, and the interviewer may assume that that is personal income when it is actually family income.

Ambiguity is not, however, restricted to direct communication between researchers and respondents. If researchers have observed the behavior of an individual and have used that behavior to infer unobserved aspects of the individual, their conclusions may be incorrect due to ambiguity. For example, the absenteeism among clerical workers may be assumed to indicate poor morale when it is actually due to a flu epidemic which has hit the public schools.

Managers should be able to determine whether ambiguity is likely to reduce the meaningfulness of a research report by evaluating the methodology used to obtain the data. *In the case of personal or telephone interviews, only trained personnel should be used* to ensure that the questions asked were clear and that the answers were properly understood and not shaped by the words or actions of the interviewer. *Written questionnaires should be pretested,* that is, preliminarily administered to a small but representative sample as a basis for revising ambiguous questions. Even when observational studies are involved, ambiguity can be reduced. For example, quantity and quality of work can be evaluated along with absenteeism as indicators of morale.

Ambiguity tends to cause problems of unreliability. In the income question example, ambiguity may cause researchers to overstate the income for some respondents and understate it for others.

A more serious problem is *wording bias* because it produces inaccurate responses that consistently tend to either overstate or understate the true response. The free-trade surveys discussed at the beginning of the first chapter illustrate the way in which wording can dramatically alter survey results.

The following questions are taken from three national surveys and intentionally attempt to bias the results:

• Should Congress make huge cuts in defense spending which would jeopardize the development of new defense systems such as the B-1 bomber and the cruise missile?

• Are you in favor of allowing construction union czars the power to shut down an entire construction site because of a dispute with a single contractor . . . thus forcing even more workers to knuckle under to union agents?

• Do you believe that private citizens have the right to own firearms to defend themselves, their families, and their property from violent criminal attack?

The bias in these questions is easily seen in the fact that it is possible to guess what answer the survey designers want the respondents to give. It is obvious that the designers are hoping for the answer *no* to the first two questions and *yes* to the third.

The bias comes through the use of words which are emotionally charged, such as *huge cuts* rather than simply *cuts* and *union czars* rather than *union leaders.* As well, questions can bias responses by providing editorial comments to the basic question. The third question not only asks about the right to own firearms but goes on to suggest how the guns might be used by law-abiding citizens. It does not point out any of the unlawful but, unfortunately, popular alternative uses which persuade some individuals to support gun control.

Managers should be highly suspicious of research reports which do not include a copy of the questionnaire. A careful examination of the questionnaire for possible wording bias is mandatory when the researchers are not under the control of the managers and have a stake in the outcome of the decision about to be made. This certainly should have been the case with the three surveys represented above, as they were used to shape public policy. It is also important even when the research effort is most conscientious because questions may be inadvertently biased, as was the free-trade question used in the *New York Times* survey discussed in Chapter 1.

Steps can also be taken to eliminate such bias from a study. Relatively neutral words can be substituted for emotionally charged ones. If this is not possible, then two versions of a question can be given to separate subsamples of the respondents, and the results of the two can be combined so that the biases in each are offsetting.

In a survey on television advertising, I found that 62 percent of one subsample of respondents felt that the federal government "should not allow" television advertising to be directed toward children. In contrast, 46 percent of a second subsample felt that the federal government should "forbid" such advertising. The reason for the discrepancy is that respondents tend to be reluctant to use the word *forbid.* The truly unbiased percentage is probably closer to the 62 percent figure but can be estimated by averaging the two figures.

A third type of measurement error due to an improperly designed scale is referred to here as specification error. *Specification error* exists if the assumptions required in order to summarize data with a quantitative model are not met. Specification error is a term commonly applied to poor econometric models, but it is used somewhat more broadly here.

The models referred to can incorporate one or several variables. An example of a model involving a single variable is where the mean, or arithmetic average, is used to represent the general level of income in a city. An assumption of the model, which is met in this case, is that the individual incomes can be represented precisely in a quantitative manner.

The use of the mean would not be appropriate to summarize the average ranking of a set of political candidates because the number 1 ranking might be assigned by one respondent to indicate who was the best of a group of very good candidates; the second respondent might give the same rank to the same candidate but feel that the candidate is the best of a sorry lot and plan not to vote for any of them.

The use of even the simplest quantitative model is questionable when subjective items are being measured, such as the attitudes and opinions of respondents. Most people may be able to say with ease that they prefer a Mercedes-Benz to a Volkswagen, but they would probably find it very difficult to make the precise statement that they prefer the Mercedes, say, 2.78 times as much as the Volkswagen. If such difficulties exist with the use of simple models, then they are compounded when more complex models are employed.

Specification error is a common problem when more complex models utilizing several variables are used to summarize data. An example of such a model would be a simple linear regression:

$$\hat{Y} = -a + bx,$$

where $\hat{Y}$ represents the predicted amount of total savings of a family and x represents the family's income. The negative value of the a coefficient indicates that at very low levels of income, families do not save (and they dip into savings if they have any). The positive b coefficient indicates that (beyond the minimum income level), increases in income will produce constant increases in savings. For example, a coefficient of .20 would indicate that the average family saves 20 percent of its income.

Specification error occurs if any of the assumptions underlying this simple model are violated. For example, the variables used in the model must be measured in a proper quantitative manner. This is not likely to be a problem in this example with the measurement of income and savings. Also, it is assumed that the functional form of the model is correct. This is questionable in the example because the percentage of income saved generally increases with the level of income. A third assumption is that all of the variables necessary to account for the differences in the spending levels of families have been included in the model. This is clearly questionable in this case. Other factors which might be included are the size of the family, the stage of the family in the family life cycle, and expectations for future earnings.

The use of sophisticated statistical models is often justified because of the complexity of the business problem being studied. However, the appropriateness of a model in a particular set of circumstances should be considered carefully. *An understanding of the technical assumptions underlying statistical models is usually outside the area of expertise and interest of most managers, but they can ask the researchers to enumerate the assumptions involved in a particular analysis and indicate the extent to which each one is realistic.*

• MEASUREMENT ERROR DUE TO AN IMPROPERLY USED SCALE

As was stated earlier, measurement error can also occur because a scale is improperly used. *Inaccuracy* is the term commonly associated with the latter type of measurement error; it refers to the instance where information has been received incorrectly from the respondent or recorded incorrectly by the researcher.

Inaccurate statements about the past, present, or future can be made by the respondent because of either an unwillingness or an inability to provide correct information. For example, a man reveals that he has a certain amount of insurance but has forgotten about a small policy obtained through his company. A homemaker indicates during a telephone interview that her favorite magazine is *Harper's* when it is really *True Story*. A sales representative incorrectly estimates what her sales for the next year will be simply because she has no real basis for knowing. A lower-level manager indicates in an application for a management training program that he will be with the company for the next year, when actually he is looking for a job.

Although inaccuracy due to inability is straightforward, inaccuracy due to unwillingness can occur for a number of reasons. The length of the interview or questionnaire may be such that the respondents provide superficial answers to the questions. Respondents may wish to create a feeling of prestige or status rather than reflect their true feelings. Likewise, respondents may provide incorrect answers based on the feeling that the subject involved is a private matter and is not the business of the researchers. Finally, respondents may simply provide answers which they feel will conform to the expectations of the researchers. This is a particular problem in such societies as Japan, where respondents consider critical comments even in an interview to be impolite.

Inaccuracy can also occur due to inability or unwillingness on the part of the researchers. Perhaps the most common problem exists with the simple act of recording the data and preparing it for analysis. Such errors tend to accumulate in a study that is not carefully conducted and can wash out subtle findings. Equally dangerous is the tendency for interviewers to influence the respondents to provide answers which are consistent with their own personal views or their expectations of how the respondents should think and behave. For example, an interviewer with liberal political beliefs may either consciously or unconsciously encourage respondents who are also liberal and discourage those of a conservative nature.

• CONCLUSION

Instrument validity and instrument reliability are the two standards by which measurement instruments are most commonly judged. It is a reasonable expectation of managers that the measures they use in research reports are sufficiently valid that there is a basic correlation between the scores assigned to individuals or objects and the true scores. As well, these scores should be sufficiently reliable that it is possible to make meaningful distinctions among objects or across situations based on differences in scores.

Measurement error can occur either because a scale has been improperly designed or because it is improperly used. The problems commonly confronted in the design of a scale involve ambiguity, wording bias, and specification error. The basic problem confronted in the measurement process is inaccuracy due to the inability or unwillingness of the respondent or the researcher.

Where human attitudes, opinions, or behavior are involved, it is impossible to eliminate measurement error. However, significant steps can be taken to reduce it substantially. A careful examination of the scaling and measurement efforts of researchers is mandatory to ensure that the existence of quality measures is not simply an article of faith. In instances where the researchers or the sponsors of research have a stake in the outcome of the decisions involved, it is especially important to ensure that intentional bias does not exist.

CHAPTER 4

Ensuring that Sample-Based Findings Can Be Generalized

Figures often beguile me, particularly when I have the arranging of them myself; in which case the remark attributed to Disraeli would often apply with justice and force: There are three kinds of lies: lies, damned lies, and statistics.

Mark Twain

He uses statistics as a drunkard uses a lamppost, for support, not for illumination.

G. K. Chesterton

This chapter presents four errors—frame, nonresponse, selection, and sampling—which limit researchers' ability to apply results based upon a sample to the larger group of interest. It is important that managers recognize all of these errors because researchers will often devote their attention to sampling error to the exclusion of the other three. One reason for this is that *sampling error is the only one of the many forms of error discussed in this book that can be estimated with any real precision.* A second reason is that some researchers use statistical analysis to intimidate managers and distract their attention from more severe limitations of their work—in the same manner that a magician uses his empty hand to distract the attention of the audience from the other hand, which is actually performing the deception.

Most of the time, researchers conduct studies utilizing samples from which they attempt to make generalizations about the full population of concern. Marketing managers, for example, develop marketing plans concerning over 80 million households based on conclusions drawn from the study of a sample of a few thousand households. To do otherwise would require more time and money than they can afford. The U.S. government, in its census of population, attempts such a complete enumeration of a population. The census of 1980 took several years to organize and complete, and it cost over a billion dollars. Even then the number of lawsuits concerning the accuracy of the results suggests that the effort was less than perfect—at least in the eyes of some.

At times, researchers may even sacrifice a larger sample size for gains in other areas. For example, a study involving 500 personal interviews might be preferred over one involving 1,000 telephone interviews because it may be felt that the gain from reducing measurement error more than offsets the loss due to an increase in sampling error.

Inferential statistics is a body of knowledge concerning the estimation of sampling error—the discrepancy between an estimate of a variable calculated from a sample and the true value for a population. Of the many errors which may be encountered in business research, sampling error is the only one that can be measured with any precision. However, there are three other types of error which also limit the generalizability of sample results—frame error, nonresponse error, and selection error. Sections of this chapter are devoted to each of these errors as well as to sampling error. The final section illustrates these four errors and measurement error by discussing their impact on the estimation of the unemployment rate by the Bureau of the Census.

• FRAME ERROR

Attitudes toward the municipal government in a medium-sized city were assessed by telephone interviews of 950 voters selected randomly from the phone book. The results suggested that the respondents in general were satisfied with the local government and that upper-income homeowners were particularly pleased. The researcher had to qualify these findings, however, by pointing out that the favorable results were due, at least in part, to problems inherent in the use of the telephone book in selecting the sample. On the one hand, people who were not homeowners or who were not in the upper-income segments tended to view the government less favorably but were not well represented in the telephone book: the young, the old, students, and minorities. On the other hand, people who were listed in the phone book but who lived outside the city limits tended to respond favorably because they enjoyed the city's services without the burden of its taxes.

This particular problem is called frame error. A *frame* is a master list used to enumerate all of the elements in the population under study. A frame is inaccurate either because it excludes elements that are a part of the population or because it includes elements that are not. Even if managers wished to interview all of the individuals in the population of interest, an inaccurate frame would prevent them from doing so. The researcher might actually contact everyone in the frame and only reach a percentage of the population. As many as one third of the households with telephones have either unlisted numbers or incorrectly listed numbers in some phone books. Also, as many as 10 percent of the households simply do not have phones, and the percentage is far higher in other parts of the world.

If the population of households was fairly homogeneous, then the inability to reach a third or more would not be a major problem; it would be a random form of error which could simply be treated as sampling error. However, the real danger of frame error comes when (1) the frame is inaccurate and (2) there are systematic differences among those accurately included in the frame, on the one hand, and those who are inaccurately excluded or included, on the other hand. This leads to a systematic form of error which is very dangerous.

Thus, an important factor in good research is the selection or development of the most accurate frame possible. Companies specialize in the sale of mailing lists, or frames, which can be used to reach specialized groups. When such a frame is unavailable it is possible to use a larger one which includes the target population, and questions can be asked to isolate respondents of interest. On written questionnaires this involves the use of *filter questions,* and it is referred to as *qualifying the respondent* in telephone and personal interviews. For example, individuals selected randomly from the telephone books of major U.S. cities were qualified as regular moviegoers before being interviewed about the movie *Superman.* This was necessary because no list of individuals who attended the movie existed.

A technique commonly used to reduce frame error associated with the use of the phone book is referred to as *random-digit dialing.* There are several methods, but one involves selecting numbers from the directory, adding "1" to them and calling the new number. Thus, if 454-5355 were selected, 454-5356 would be called. This procedure produces listed and unlisted households in the same proportion that they exist in the area. It does not eliminate the problem of frame error because of the households which do not have a phone. However, random-digit dialing will make a substantial reduction in the problem.

Once a survey has been conducted, managers should ask three questions. First, *how substantial is the inaccuracy of the frame?* For example, the use of the firms listed on the New York Stock Exchange for a frame in a study of the relationship between monetary policy and stock prices would obviously exclude firms listed on the other exchanges. Second, *are there likely to be any systematic differences between the types of individuals or objects inappropriately excluded or included and those which are accurately included?* This would obviously be the case for the study of stock prices, as only the larger and older firms are listed in the exchange. Third, *given the answers to the first two questions, in what manner and to what degree should the results be qualified?* For example, it might be felt that smaller firms would be more susceptible to changes in monetary policy than the larger and generally more diversified firms listed on the Exchange.

• NONRESPONSE ERROR

Even if researchers were able to design a perfect measurement instrument and conduct a census using a frame which was perfectly accurate, they would still have to contend with nonresponse error. The fact that researchers attempt to contact every potential respondent does not guarantee that everyone is able or willing to respond. In a telephone survey, some potential respondents will not be found at home and others will refuse to participate. If those who participate are representative of those who do not, then the researchers will be faced with another random form of error similar to sampling error. However, those who do respond are often quite different from those who do not. For example, the elderly are more likely to be at home and thus be able to respond to a telephone survey than those who work. Also, if a survey investigates some controversial issue, those who are strongly in favor of it and those who are strongly against it are generally more likely to respond than those who do not feel strongly about the issue. Additionally, a higher percentage of middle-class subjects respond to surveys than their upper- and lower-class counterparts. Thus, *nonresponse error exists when: (1) less than 100 percent of those the researchers attempt to contact respond to a survey, and (2) there is a systematic difference in the responses of those who have and those who have not responded.*

The potential impact of nonresponse error on research results can be quite significant, as Table 4.1 indicates. If researchers have a response rate of 40 percent (row 3), and 50 percent of those responding say yes to a yes/no question (column 3), then the percent saying

TABLE 4.1

The Potential Influence of Nonresponse on the Answers to Yes/No Questions

Rate of Return (R)	Proportion of Respondents Saying Yes to a Yes/No Question (Y)				
	.05	.25	.50	.75	.90
.90	.05–.15	.23–.33	.45–.55	.68–.78	.81–.91
.60	.03–.43	.15–.55	.30–.70	.45–.85	.54–.94
.40	.02–.62	.10–.70	.20–.80	.30–.90	.36–.96
.20	.01–.81	.05–.85	.10–.90	.15–.95	.18–.98

Table reads: The entries are calculated where the lower limit is RY and the upper limit is $1 - R(1 - Y)$.

yes for all potential respondents could be as low as 20 percent or as high as 80 percent.

Nonresponse error is generally greater for mail questionnaires than for either telephone or personal interviews. A response rate of less than 25 percent is not uncommon, although substantially higher percentages can be achieved. In a survey conducted by army psychologists, an enlisted man refused to respond. After repeated requests, the psychologists went to his commanding officer, who also requested unsuccessfully that he complete the questionnaire. The enlisted man was later court-martialed for refusing the officer's direct order to complete the questionnaire. Rarely do researchers have such power over respondents, so a great deal of guile is often used to increase the response rate, and much research has been conducted on the problem. Most of this research has involved mail surveys, and one finding is that surveys using first class mail tend to do better than those using bulk rate postage, probably because the latter surveys are viewed as "junk mail."

• SELECTION ERROR

The researchers conducting the beer taste tests described in Chapter 2 rented a store on a busy street in a major city and, over a period of several weeks, recruited 500 subjects from the adult males who passed by. It is quite unlikely that such a sampling procedure would ever provide a representative cross-section of the population because not all types of people are equally likely to be walking down any one street. Also, as the rumor got out that "they're passing out free beer down on Simon Avenue," the population of drunks, derelicts, and college students would probably increase significantly. With such a poor sampling procedure, an unrepresentative sample of 500 respondents would not provide a significant improvement over an estimate based on an unrepresentative sample of 100, and both would be significantly inferior to a representative sample of 50.

Selection error occurs if some of the elements in the frame have a greater probability of being included in the sample than others, and this fact is not accounted for in the analysis. Such an error will cause a biased result.

Sampling

There are two basic types of sampling procedures: probability and nonprobability.

1. In *probability sampling,* every element in the frame has a known chance of being selected for inclusion in the sample. The simple random sample is an example of a probability sample, where the probability of choosing an element is not only known but is the same for all units. The simple random sample may be viewed from the perspective of the samples drawn from the larger population or from the perspective of the individual elements which make up these samples. If researchers are drawing a sample of 1,000 from a population of 1,000,000, there is a very large number of unique combinations of sampling units available for selection. If the sampling procedure is truly random, then each of these combinations has the same probability of being selected as the sample.

Viewed from the perspective of the individual sampling unit, a sampling procedure is random if each unit has an equal chance of being selected. Thus each unit has a chance in a million of being selected. (As a technical aside, this view of the random sample does not make the distinction between sampling with and without replacement of the sampling units. Most research in business research employs sampling without replacement as elements of the population cannot appear in the sample more than once. However, it is generally a distinction of little practical importance and can be left to the researchers to worry about.)

Not all probability sampling procedures are designed to give elements of the population an equal probability of being included in the sample. For example, researchers may choose to use *stratified sampling* in doing a survey of businesses. The population businesses could be divided into three subpopulations based on the size of the businesses. A proportionally large sample could be selected from the stratum containing the large businesses and proportionally smaller samples could be selected for the two smaller strata. Although the probability of selecting a particular business depends on its size, that probability is known. Thus, a weighted average of the three separate estimates can be calculated, and sampling error can be estimated.

2. In *nonprobability sampling,* the probability that an element is included in the sample is neither equal nor known for all elements. Some mechanism other than chance is used to select the sample. In the case of the beer study mentioned earlier in the chapter, the criterion for selecting the sample seemed to be the convenience of the researchers rather than the representativeness of the sample finally chosen. After a survey was conducted in a southwestern city with a significant Spanish- speaking population, it was discovered that the interviewers who did not speak Spanish tended to skip the families with Spanish surnames in the selection for the sampling. This meant that nonprobability sampling was actually being used.

The procedures used to measure sampling error have traditionally required a random sample but have been modified to accommodate other probability sampling techniques. However, sampling error cannot be measured if a nonprobability sampling technique is employed. This is not to say that sampling error is always greater when a nonprobability sampling procedure is used. The problem is that there is simply no basis for measuring the selection error that exists.

The distinction between probability and nonprobability sampling procedures can be illustrated by comparing the way in which a pollster and a newspaper reporter would go about assessing public opinion before an election. The pollster might have a group of trained interviewers administer a written questionnaire to a sample of 1,200 households selected randomly from the phone book, using random-digit dialing, and summarize the responses quantitatively. The use of the random sample means that there is no danger of selection error and that sampling error can be measured.

In contrast, a newspaper reporter might select a few individuals who, in his view, are opinion leaders that speak for the community, as well as a few ordinary individuals, interview them in an informal fashion, and summarize their views qualitatively. The quality of the reporter's results may be as good or better than the results provided by the pollster, but there is no way of telling. There is always the danger that the reporter's judgment was bad and the individuals selected did not speak for the community at large. Unfortunately, because the sample was selected subjectively, it must also be evaluated subjectively.

Thus, *the use of nonprobability sampling procedures creates two problems: (1) It introduces the potential for selection error and thus, the danger that the sample will be unrepresentative. (2) If selection error exists, then it is impossible for sampling error to be measured,* and the procedures discussed in the next section cannot be applied.

Selection error as it has been discussed so far exists

if an unrepresentative sample has been drawn because of the use of a nonprobability sampling procedure. It will also exist if a sample is drawn from one population and the results are used to make generalizations about another population. For example, a random sample of Fortune 500 executives can be used to generalize about all Fortune 500 executives, but it cannot be used to generalize about all American business executives. The rule is that *it is possible to make inferences about a population with sample data only if it is based on a probability sample of that population.*

Despite the fact that nonprobability samples are suspect, there are instances when their use may be appropriate. First, in the qualitative phase of research, the individuals selected for in-depth interviews or to participate in focus groups are usually selected judgmentally, as was pointed out in Chapter 2. However, it is important that this research be followed up with a quantitative research phase where a probability sampling procedure is employed.

Second, if the population is homogeneous, then a sample drawn on the basis of convenience is as good as a random sample. This is why physicians don't have to prick us in various parts of our bodies in drawing a blood sample. It is also why the product testing done by Consumer's Union does not attempt to give all of the products of the same brand an equal chance of being in a test.

Third, researchers may opt to use a nonprobability sample when budget or time constraints are so severe that the alternative is to do no research at all.

Fourth, if the problem is a minor one or the decision maker is casual about it, then a nonprobability sample may be drawn. Thus, a business will rarely give a convention hotel a second chance if the service was bad the first time. It is also interesting to consider that the spouse selection decision often involves a set of very unscientific sampling (and measurement) procedures; most of the individuals I know (a highly nonrandom sample) have selected highly nonrandom samples (of varying size) of members (of varying size) of the opposite sex to date and have shown little regard for candid and unambiguous communication.

• SAMPLING ERROR

Sampling error occurs whenever inferences are made about characteristics of a population by examining a sample of it rather than the whole thing. In the discussion of specification error in the previous chapter, it was suggested that univariate, bivariate, or multivariate models can be used to summarize data. Sampling error exists when these models are fit to sample data and these fitted models are used to describe the population from which the sample was taken. If the average price for a random sample of 300 stocks for the New York Stock Exchange is $56.78 and the average price is actually $65.89 (these numbers are precise but inaccurate), then sampling error is equal to the difference of $9.11.

Figure 4.1 illustrates the way in which sampling error varies with the sample size employed. Suppose that researchers are attempting to estimate with sample data some unknown percentage describing the full population, and suppose that the actual value is 50 percent (represented by the horizontal line in the middle of the figure). The horizontal axis represents the various sample sizes that might be employed. The vertical axis represents the possible sample estimates and ranges from 0 percent to 100 percent. If researchers utilize a random sample, then 99 percent of all of the sample estimates will fall between the two curved lines which converge as the sample size increases.

Thus, the fact that the two lines converge means that sample estimates are becoming better and better as the sample size is increased. If researchers employ a sample size of 50, then 99 percent of the time researchers will receive sample estimates between 31.8 and 68.2 percent. If they employ a sample size of 1,000, then 99 percent of the time they will receive sample estimates between 46 and 54 percent.

FIGURE 4.1

Variability of Sample Estimates Decreases as Sample Size Increases

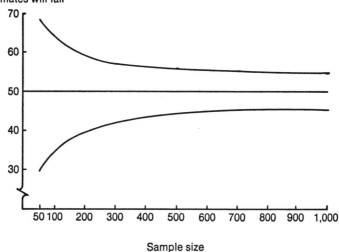

Range in which
99% of sample
estimates will fall

Sample size

A discussion of the selection of a sample size certainly goes beyond the domain of this book, but some general comments can be made. The size of a sample can be evaluated both in an absolute sense and relative to the size of the population from which the sample is drawn.

First, *a sample size of less than 35 is generally too small to be of much use in evaluating sampling error.* Several years ago I was invited to a luncheon held by a computer software firm for a candidate for the directorship of marketing research. The candidate described the surveys he had conducted of software users, which typically had a sample size of around 35. It might have helped him to know of an exercise I use with undergraduate marketing research students.

I give each student a random sample of 35 questionnaires taken from an actual survey, which employed a much larger sample size, and ask them to see if there is a relationship between the respondents' income levels and their consumption of fresh oranges. Typically, half conclude that no relationship exists and the others say there is one. Of those finding a relationship, half say that lower-income respondents are more likely to consume fresh oranges and the other half say that higher-income respondents do. I then proceed to a discussion of statistical inference.

Second, *the size of the population generally has little influence upon the amount of sampling error associated with a particular sample size* because most populations are extremely large from a technical point of view. Although it is not very intuitive, a sample size of 100 selected from a city of 100,000 will produce results which essentially are as good as they would be from a city of 10,000,000.

Third, *an exception to the previous rules occurs when the sample size is "large" relative to the population size, say, greater than half a percent.* Thus, a sample size of 100 in a town of 1,000 would be better than in the larger cities. As well, a sample of a 100 in a village of 100 would constitute a census, and no sampling error would be involved. When such situations hold, the conventional formulas for measuring sampling must be modified slightly.

Measuring Sampling Error

There are two ways in which sampling error is measured—parameter estimation and hypothesis testing. In *parameter estimation,* researchers allow for sampling error without incorporating their expectations concerning the true value of the parameter being estimated. In *hypothesis testing,* they evaluate a sample estimate and the possible impact sampling error may have by comparing it to their expectation about the true value of the parameter.

Suppose that researchers interviewed a number of purchasing agents and found that 56 percent of them indicated that their level of buying activity would increase during the next quarter. If they evaluated this sample statistic with parameter estimation they might say that the estimate is 56 percent plus or minus 3 percentage points at the .95 percent confidence level. What this means is that the best estimate of the population parameter is 56 percent, but that this is not precise because of sampling error, and thus there is a .95 chance that the true value actually lies between 53 and 59 percent. Alternatively, there is a .05 percent chance that the sample estimate will be off by more than 3 percentage points.

It is important that a research report provide both the confidence level and confidence interval (the plus or minus figure) when presenting a sample mean or percent. Notice that Table 1.1 said that the results are "accurate to within plus or minus 6 percentage points." This does not say very much because the confidence level might be .50, suggesting that there was a .50 chance that the true percentage being estimated could be off by more than 6 percentage points.

Another misleading thing about this statement is that it talks about sampling error as if it were the only form of error, since it speaks generally about accuracy. Unfortunately, there are other more significant problems with the study, such as the poorly worded question. This illustrates why it can be said that just as a magician may use one hand conspicuously to conceal what is going on with the other, so a researcher may use an elaborate discussion of statistics to distract the report reader's attention from errors more significant than sampling.

The second method of evaluating sampling error is through *hypothesis testing.* Hypothesis testing could be used to evaluate the results of the survey of purchasing agents discussed above. The researchers would begin with an expectation concerning the percentage of purchasing agents who indicate that their buying will increase in the next quarter. For example, they might hypothesize that the true percentage is 50 for the full population. The survey would be used to confirm or disconfirm this hypothesis.

As the survey result was 56 percent, there is a discrepancy of 6 percentage points. According to the theory underlying hypothesis testing procedure, this discrepancy has two possible explanations. First, the hypothesis is good and the sample estimate is bad because of sampling error. Second, the sample estimate is good and the hypothesis is bad.

The relative plausibility of these two explanations is influenced by several factors. If the sample size is large, then more faith can be placed in the sample estimate. Thus, the discrepancy of 6 percentage points may not be significant with a sample size of 100; it probably is if the sample size is 2,000. Also, the plausibility of the two explanations for the discrepancy depends upon its size, as large discrepancies are increasingly difficult to dismiss as being due to sampling error. Thus, a difference between the hypothesized value and the sample value of 6 percentage points may be attributed to sampling error if the sample size is 100, while a difference of 66 percentage points probably cannot be.

Hypothesis testing quantifies these and other considerations into a formal evaluation of the possibility that discrepancies between hypothesized and sample values are due to sampling error (referred to as the null hypothesis). In the process, there are two dangers:

1. Sampling error can create a large artificial difference between the hypothesized and sample values, causing researchers to falsely assume that the hypothesis is bad (statisticians refer to this as a Type I error). This would be the case if survey results showed that 60 percent of the purchasing agents indicated that they would buy more, when the hypothesized value of 50 percent was actually correct.

2. Sampling error might conceal differences between the hypothesized and sample values, causing researchers to falsely assume that the hypothesis is good (a Type

II error). If the survey results were 51 percent and the hypothesized value was 50 percent, then the researchers might assume incorrectly that the hypothesized value was good. The likelihood that either of these mistakes occurs declines as the sample size increases.

Hypothesis testing exists in many forms. It can also be used to compare a sample mean against a hypothesized value or the parameters of a regression based on sample data against the hypothesis that no relationship exists. Additionally, hypothesis testing can be used to determine if two populations can be described with identical univariate, bivariate, or multivariate models. The simplest case would occur where researchers evaluate the ratings provided by a sample of respondents who tried a carbonated drink sweetened with sugar with the ratings provided by another sample who tried the same carbonated drink artificially sweetened.

• ERRORS IN ESTIMATING THE U.S. UNEMPLOYMENT RATE

Most of the time when the quantitative results of research are presented, there is a danger that the errors of measurement, frame, nonresponse, and sampling error will have been involved at least to some degree. Measurement error will exist if there have been problems with either the design or use of the measurement instruments used to produce the quantitative results. Frame, nonresponse, selection, and sampling error will likely present problems if less than 100 percent of the target population is involved in a study, which is virtually always the case in practice.

The common presence of these errors and the problems they can cause can be illustrated by reviewing the way the U.S. unemployment rate is calculated. This, as well as most other economic statistics, is calculated by the Bureau of the Census, which does the most expensive and probably the finest economic research in the country.

The unemployment rate is calculated monthly from a survey consisting of personal interviews of approximately 60,000 households. The individual households are selected using a stratified sampling procedure, which ensures that all of the hundreds of geographic areas for which the statistics are calculated are adequately represented in every survey.

Special effort is taken to ensure that measurement error is minimized. Interviewers receive continual training and are under close supervision while in the field. A subsample of respondents is reinterviewed by the supervisors to guarantee that correct information has been obtained in each interview.

More problems seem to exist concerning the design of the measurement instruments to measure unemployment than in the use of these instruments. The basic problems involve the definitions used. The *unemployment rate* is the percent of the *work force* which is *unemployed*. Recently, individuals in the military were excluded from the work force, so the new measure tends to understate (at least by historical standards) the unemployment rate by reducing the denominator of the fraction. Also, the fact that those who have not looked for work in the past four months are not considered to be part of the work force tends to exclude the chronically unemployed, thereby understating the unemployment problem.

Fewer problems exist with the generalization of findings based on the sample to the full work force. Frame error is not a significant problem because sample households are selected on the basis of their physical location, and thus there is no dependence on any list which might become inaccurate. Nonresponse error is minimized through personal interviews, and the nonresponse rate is held at 3 to 5 percent. Selection error is eliminated because of the probability sampling procedure used.

Sampling error is relatively small, by conventional standards, because of the large sample size employed. Parameter estimation is used to represent sampling error, a confidence level of .90, and the corresponding confidence interval of plus or minus .12 percent. Thus, if the estimated unemployment rate is 9 percent, there is a .90 probability that the true percent is between 8.88 percent and 9.12 percent.

Having to allow for sampling error by only plus or minus .12 percent is extraordinarily good but translates into an error rate of plus or minus 122,000 unemployed workers. When the other four errors are considered, the total error rate is even greater, as those who administer unemployment funds to individuals are often very much aware.

• CONCLUSION

Although the four types of error discussed in this chapter and measurement error, discussed in the previous chapter, are similar in that they all tend to undermine the meaningfulness of research results, they are distinct and must be dealt with in different ways. Researchers can:

1. Minimize measurement error by working to guarantee that the measurement instruments are properly designed and used.

2. Reduce frame error by ensuring that the frame used has few improper inclusions or exclusions.

3. Decrease nonresponse error by seeing to it that everyone has an adequate chance of being contacted and that those who are contacted are encouraged to participate.

4. Eliminate selection error by taking a census or, if that is impossible, by taking a probability rather than a nonprobability sample.

5. Eliminate sampling error also by taking a census, and if that is impossible, then it can be controlled for by selecting the most appropriate probability sampling technique and using a large sample size.

It is interesting to consider that so much attention is placed on the measurement of sampling error when the impact of the four other forms of error are at least as great. As was mentioned earlier in the chapter, that may be simply because sampling error is relatively easy to measure.

CHAPTER 5

Ensuring that Causal Inferences Are Supported

It is now proved beyond doubt that smoking is one of the leading causes of statistics.

Reader's Digest

A statistician is a man who comes to the rescue of figures that cannot lie for themselves.

Evan Esar

Purposeful human activity is based on two rather heroic assumptions. The first is that our actions have an influence on the world around us and thus on our fates. The second is that our understanding of the complex system of causes and effects which make up our world is sufficiently accurate that our actions improve our condition at least marginally.

The succession of successes and failures which make up both our individual histories and the history of the human race provides strong support for the first of these assumptions and little for the second. No doubt future generations will look upon some current medical practice as we look upon bleeding and applying leeches to patients. Public school students will suffer from some wonderful new pedagogical approach as their parents suffered from "new math." Modern management practices will probably come to be considered just as naive as the "scientific management" of Taylor is today.

The basic dilemma is that we must make decisions on a day-to-day basis and for each we must assume a particular causal relationship between the decision alternatives we face (referred to by researchers as the independent variable) and the possible outcomes of that decision (the dependent variable). Unfortunately, we have often been either unable or unwilling to go to the trouble to establish true causal relations before acting.

This chapter begins with an elementary discussion of the ways in which causal relations are established, and it goes on to discuss the types of error encountered when such relations are not established properly.

• ESTABLISHING CAUSALITY

For some time I drove a 20-year-old Jaguar which had a dead spot in its starter. Each morning it would take me several attempts to get it started. But once I turned the key to the proper position, it would start every time. One day I took the car to be serviced, and the mechanic pointed out that there was a leak in the fuel line. Once the fuel line was repaired, the problem with the starter mysteriously disappeared.

While I labeled my behavior as stupidity, a philosopher would probably be more gracious and say that I had committed the logical fallacy of *post hoc, ergo propter hoc,* literally meaning "after this, therefore because of this." In other words, just because one event follows another does not mean that it is caused by it. This explains why economists can argue for contradictory economic policies, with each one finding support for his or her point of view in the same set of data.

There are actually three sets of circumstances in which empirical evidence can be found to support a conclusion concerning the causal relationship between two variables. The weakest is when a simple *association* is found between two variables. There is a study, probably apocryphal, which concluded that milk consumption prevents cancer. The conclusion was based on a large, negative, and statistically significant correlation between incidence of milk consumption and that of cancer for a large sample of individuals. Thus, those who drank milk tended not to have the disease, while those who did not drink it tended to have it.

One problem with this finding is that it does not account for the age of the individuals in the study. Young people tend to drink more milk and have fewer illnesses than older people. In fact, the same statistical argument could probably be used to demonstrate that bed-wetting prevents both cancer and high personal incomes.

Luckily these false causal statements are implausible even though they may be consistent with empirical findings of association. *The real problem comes when false causal statements are both plausible and consistent with findings of association.* The fact that a management policy works in one environment and not in another may suggest that more important factors are not being considered. The same difficulty exists with much medical research. One study finds that coffee consumption leads to heart disease while another finds that it does not. Although both studies may be accurate in terms of the errors discussed in the previous chapters, they are inconsistent insofar as their causal implications are concerned: coffee either is or is not a cause of heart disease.

Suppose that researchers did a study using a random sample of postal employees and found that there was a strong, positive, and statistically significant correlation between morale and productivity. There are three causal explanations consistent with this finding: (1) high morale caused high productivity; (2) high productivity caused high morale; and (3) some other factor, such as level of training, caused both high morale and high productivity.

If no correlation had been found, it would not have been possible to argue that high morale causes high productivity. However, the fact that the study found a positive correlation between morale and productivity is of limited value because the results are consistent with all three of these rival explanations. Thus, it can be said that association is necessary but not sufficient in drawing conclusions concerning the nature of causal relationships between variables.

A second, somewhat stronger, basis for establishing causality is to identify a *sequence of events* between variables. If a study of postal workers finds that the productivity of workers with high morale tends to increase over time and that the morale of workers with high productivity does not tend to increase over time, then the support is consistent with the first explanation listed above and inconsistent with the second. Thus, one of the rival explanations consistent with the association has been ruled out by identifying the sequence of events between the two variables.

A problem still remains in that both the second and third explanations are consistent with the particular sequence of events found. One approach would be to try to determine what other factor might influence both morale and productivity, then measure this factor and incorporate this measure into a statistical model such as multiple regression. In fact, a number of additional factors can be treated in this manner.

The problem remaining is specification error (discussed in Chapter 3). One can never be absolutely certain that all of the relevant additional factors have been incorporatcd into the model or that the functional form of the model properly expresses the relationships among the variables included in it.

Although establishing a sequence of events in searching for the causal relationship between variables is superior to establishing a simple association, both approaches suffer from the same limitation: neither of them can rule out all of the rival causal explanations. If researchers are unable to identify an association or sequence of events between variables, then obviously no claims can be made regarding causality. However, finding such evidence does not establish which of the rival explanations is correct.

The third set of circumstances in which causal inferences can be drawn is where no rival explanations exist for explaining the relationship between one variable and another. In practice, this can only be achieved through the use of a controlled experiment which is discussed in the next section.

• RESEARCH DESIGNS FOR ESTABLISHING CAUSALITY

Although the topic of designing research is extremely complex, three major types of studies are employed in business research and elsewhere. The first is a *cross-sectional study*. In a cross-sectional study, data are collected at a single point in time, and possible relationships among variables are examined by comparing various segments of the group of individuals or objects being studied.

For example, researchers might draw a sample of firms listed on the New York Stock Exchange and determine what the average price-earnings ratio is on a particular day, then go on to determine if this ratio varied significantly among industry groupings. Alternatively, researchers might survey a sample of postal workers to evaluate their morale and combine these data with the workers' evaluations by their supervisors to determine if there is any correlation between morale and productivity.

From these two examples, it should be clear that a cross-sectional study is quite simple in form. It can be expanded to incorporate a number of variables into the analysis simultaneously. However, the researchers can never be certain they can incorporate all of the right variables into a model of the correct functional form. In addition, such a study can obviously never examine the sequence of events among variables. Thus, it can only establish an association between variables, which, as was discussed in the previous section, is the weakest basis for identifying causal relations.

The second type of research design in common use is the *longitudinal study*. A longitudinal study observes one or more individuals or objects by taking repeated measurements over time. By examining changes in the variables from one period to the next, researchers can isolate the existing sequence of events.

Most econometric research on the U.S. economy employs this research approach. Repeated measures are taken on the money supply, interest rates, unemployment, and other factors, and these data are incorporated into a statistical model used to make economic predictions. Researchers could also conduct a longitudinal study of the relationship between morale and productivity of postal workers by examining the same sample repeatedly over time.

Manufacturers of consumer products employ consumer panels to examine such things as the relationship between price changes in one period and changes in market share in the following period. Such a panel typically involves the use of a sample of households who complete questionnaires or diaries on a periodic basis. A. C. Nielsen determines its television program ratings by attaching electronic devices to the televisions in sample households. The company also provides a service which measures the sales and market shares of food products by taking periodic inventories in a sample of food stores. The Bureau of the Census also uses a panel to estimate the unemployment rate for the country.

Thus, the way in which researchers establish a sequence of events between variables is to conduct a longitudinal study. Although such an approach cannot establish a causal relationship, it can help to isolate one.

The third type of research design in use in business research is the *controlled experiment. Experiment* is a word in common misuse. It is used in the loose sense of trying something out—as when a teenager (or Dr. Jekyll) experiments with drugs. More appropriately, it has a more technical meaning which describes the activities a pharmaceutical company uses when developing a drug.

In a controlled experiment, researchers attempt to isolate a causal relationship by eliminating the influence of all of the factors which might tend to obscure it. In the terminology of research, eliminating the influence of these factors is referred to as controlling for them. Thus, if chemists are looking at the reaction which takes place when two compounds are mixed in varying amounts, then temperature is controlled by holding it constant across all the experimental situations. Through such control, researchers can eliminate the contaminating influence of all environmental factors which might present rival explanations for the reaction that occurred.

In most business research, control is much more difficult because of the complexity of the phenomena being studied. If researchers are interested in evaluating two methods of compensation for sales representatives, they cannot conduct repeated experimental trials with the same sales territory. The effect of the first trial will influence subsequent ones and there may be significant changes in the environment which cannot be controlled. A superior approach would be to select two sales territories which are identical in nature and environment and implement one of the methods in each. Usually, finding identical territories (or individuals or any other unit of analysis) is very difficult in practice, so it is desirable to use matched samples of territories in order to evaluate the methods of compensation.

To the extent that the individual units of analysis or samples of these units are matched, it is possible to eliminate all of the rival factors in isolating cause-effect relationships. For example, researchers might take a random sample of post offices and divide it randomly into two separate samples. A new personnel policy might be implemented in one sample in order to increase worker morale and the other sample could be left unchanged as a control group. The average productivity level could be determined for the two groups at the end of the study. To the extent that the two samples of post offices are identical in nature and environment, the impact of the induced change in morale on productivity can be determined.

Although there are many factors in the environments of the post offices, in the nature of the individual post offices, and in the individual postal workers themselves which could influence productivity, the impact of these factors is eliminated from consideration by creating the two matched groups. The beauty of such an approach is that not only are these factors automatically taken care of, but the researchers do not even have to know what they are or how they can be measured or how they should be incorporated into the analysis, as would be the case if a cross-sectional or longitudinal study were employed.

• ERRORS CONFRONTED IN DRAWING CAUSAL INFERENCES

The basic problems encountered in drawing causal inferences from research can be dramatically illustrated by a *liberal interpretation* of a study conducted at the University of California not long ago. The researchers were interested in examining the impact of jogging (the independent variable) on cardiovascular health (the dependent variable). The researchers conducted their study with a sample of Yucatan mini-swine, which are small pigs found on the Yucatan peninsula of Mexico.

The researchers took the sample of 500 Yucatan mini-swine and divided it into two groups of 250 cach. The first group was treated as an experimental group where each pig jogged on a treadmill for an average of five miles a week. The second was treated as a control group and allowed to do whatever pigs do when they are not jogging. At the end of the experiment, the researchers found that the jogging pigs were lean and svelte compared to the nonjoggers, but their cardiovascular health was no different.

Two important questions arise in evaluating these conclusions concerning the causal relationship between jogging and weight loss and cardiovascular health. First, is it true that the differences in weight and cardiovascular health between the two groups can be attributed to jogging and to no other rival explanation? Second, given a yes to the first question, can the results be generalized to other mini-swine, to other kinds of swine, or to humans?

The first of these questions addresses the internal validity of the study. A study has *internal validity* if it has been successful in eliminating all potentially confounding factors so that the true cause-effect relationship has been isolated. The second addresses the study's external validity. A study has *external validity* if the causal relationship that has been isolated can be generalized to other circumstances.

For this study to be internally valid the two groups would have to be virtually identical and be treated identically. However, there are a number of reasons why such a study could have problems with internal validity. For example, ideally the researchers should have numbered the pigs from 1 to 500 and then assigned them randomly to the two groups with the aid of the random-number generator on a computer. But, suppose that the assignment was left to a graduate student who had been out late the night before discussing the philosophy of science and did not feel very well. It was hot and the pigs smelled particularly like pigs that day.

What would be the natural tendency? He might simply select the first 250 pigs he could get his hands on and assign them to the experimental group and let the other 250 be the control group. Would there be any systematic differences between these groups which might confound the results? Certainly. The first group of pigs that was easy to catch might be made up of the aged and the infirm, while the second might consist of the wily and fleet of foot. Thus, the jogging was too little too late to do anything for the cardiovascular health of the first group, but it ruined their appetites so that they lost weight.

The question of the external validity of this study concerns whether its causal conclusions can be applied under other circumstances. To illustrate this potential problem, consider the mini-swine rancher living on a large mini-swine ranch on the Yucatan peninsula in

Mexico. He gets an order from California for 500 of his pigs. Ideally, he should use his microcomputer to select them randomly from his herd of 15,000, but it's the rainy season and they are scattered over his vast spread. He is more likely to select the first 500 his pig-hands can round up before they go off to the big little-pig rodeo.

The problem is that they round up the halt and the lame and ship them to California. Thus, the researchers unknowingly conduct their study with this unrepresentative group, and the results cannot be generalized to the young and the healthy.

I am sure that the actual study anticipated and solved these and other problems which could cause internal and external invalidity. The actual research has been abused to provide a humorous illustration of a rather dry topic. Certainly, those of us who have children born in the era of the Salk vaccine can be thankful for the internal and external validity of research on the immunization for polio which utilized animals.

There are two general situations in research where the problems of internal validity are likely to be particularly severe. In the first situation there is no control group to serve as a basis for comparison in evaluating the impact of changes in the independent variable on the dependent variable; while in the second situation there is a control group, but it is not comparable to the experimental group.

Research attempting to ascertain cause-effect relationships without the benefit of a control group is very common. This problem is characteristic of both cross-sectional and longitudinal studies. The evidence that smoking can lead to heart disease is strong, but the fact that a cross-sectional study offers findings consistent with this view is not conclusive because there are rival explanations. That smokers may be more likely to have heart disease may also be explained by the fact that they are generally older, less active, and have a different personality makeup from nonsmokers.

As well, correlational studies which indicate that firms with larger market shares have higher returns on investment do not guarantee that other firms can improve their return on investment simply by increasing market share. Other factors, such as the costs of improving products and promoting them, as well as competitive reaction to such efforts, may be important. A larger market share may be, along with a high return on investment, a measure of success and not a road to it.

Similar problems exist when researchers attempt to draw causal inferences from longitudinal studies. There are a myriad of factors which interact to make up our national economy, including the influences of the international economy on it. All of these factors operate to influence economic growth, and vice versa. Thus, it is unrealistic to conclude that any one factor is the major determinant of, or for that matter has any direct influence on, economic growth. Incidentally, an equally strong argument can be made that the historical rise in the crime rate is attributable to a coincidental rise in the consumption of sugar-coated cereals or unleaded gasoline.

A physician friend tells of a charlatan who has a clinic-resort specializing in throat problems of the wealthy and famous. An entertainer with laryngitis after a stint in Las Vegas might spend a week in the clinic, where patients are not allowed to speak and they receive esoteric and expensive treatments. My friend claims that 99 percent of laryngitis sufferers would be cured if they spent a week without talking at the Holiday Inn in Toledo.

A similar problem exists when two different and inequivalent time periods are compared. An incumbent politician will take advantage of this illogic by saying that total employment is higher and the crime rate is lower now than in the previous administration. Opposing politicians will counter with equal illogic by arguing that unemployment and serious crimes were lower in the previous administration. Both positions can be supported by the facts and neither has any merit because of the problems of internal invalidity in the longitudinal analysis.

Probably the majority of the "experiments" in business are of this uncontrolled nature. Management or outside consultants will often come up with what appears to be the solution to a personnel problem. The hypothesized solution will be implemented and then judged on the basis of the results, as if the hypothesized solution were the only factor with any influence on the success or failure of the outcome. Thus, proper solutions may be falsely rejected and poor solutions may be accepted as good ones because other forces are at work.

Most tests of new marketing efforts or new products involve such uncontrolled "experiments." A new advertising campaign may appear to have been a success because consumer demand for the product was increasing, but this may actually be due to the promotional efforts of the advertising agency which had just been fired for failure to produce instantaneous results. A potentially successful new product may not succeed in a test market only because the test had been sabotaged by a competitor with a special advertising or discounting campaign.

The second research situation likely to contain problems with internal invalidity is when the control group is not equivalent to the experimental group but is compared with it to try to isolate cause-effect relationships. This would be the problem if the slow Yucatan miniswine were placed in one group and the fast ones were placed in the other. It was also the problem in an Army field test of a prototype of a new weapon. The weapon failed in the test, and one explanation for it, which received little consideration, was that green recruits employed the experimental weapon while battle-seasoned Vietnam vets used the existing weapon, which served as a control.

Similar illogic is often used when the success of one division is attributed to its manager and the failure of another is blamed on its manager. This assumes that the manager's skill is more significant than the combined influence of all of the other factors affecting the success of a division.

This discussion is not to suggest that the addition of a control group or situation is futile unless it is perfect. It is certainly preferable to be able to evaluate results obtained from implementing a hypothesized solution to a personnel problem by comparing the department where the solution is implemented with a similar one where it is not. And if two departments can be treated as the experimental group and two as the control group, it would be even better than just using one in each group. However, to the extent to which the groups of one or more departments are not equivalent, rival explanations for the difference in the performance of the two groups should be addressed.

Problems with external invalidity can occur when researchers or managers attempt to take findings of cause-effect relationships which appear to be internally valid in one situation and apply them to another. Such problems can occur for a number of reasons:

1. The possibility that the jogging experiment was based on a sample of older mini-swine suggests that the results cannot be applied to young ones. As a rule, experimental subjects should be selected randomly from a larger population if there is a desire to generalize cause-effect conclusions to that larger population. This explains why advertising researchers must be particularly cautious in taking results which appear to be internally valid for a study conducted in New York City and trying to apply the results to the rest of the country. To do so rests on the questionable assumption that no meaningful regional differences exist.

This cause of external invalidity is quite similar to selection error, discussed in Chapter 3. Selection error occurs when research results are based upon nonprobability, and thus nonrepresentative, samples so that they do not characterize the larger population accurately. This problem can occur whether or not the objective of the study is to draw causal conclusions. For example, a simple public opinion poll can suffer from selection error, although no causal inferences are being drawn. However, if a study does attempt to draw causal inferences and suffers from selection error, then external invalidity will likely result.

2. Just as causal inferences cannot be generalized across groups, it is possible that they cannot be generalized to different times. In other words, financial strategy for a corporation which has been demonstrated to be valid in the past may not hold today because economic conditions and financial institutions have changed.

3. A final cause of external invalidity worthy of discussion here is that the research itself may alter the environment to the degree that it is no longer a part of the real world. The famous "Hawthorne effect" arose from the discovery years ago at Western Electric that workers increased their productivity no matter how they were treated simply because they knew they were being watched in an experiment.

A similar problem may exist when advertising researchers present alternative versions of print ads or television commercials to respondents and then ask these individuals to complete a questionnaire or to answer questions about the ads. The determination of the best ad among a set which the consumer has examined carefully may not be externally valid if consumers do not examine ads carefully under natural conditions.

• DISCUSSION AND CONCLUSION

Purposeful behavior in business is based on some understanding or presumption of cause-effect relations which make up the world. The available research designs vary considerably in their ability to isolate such relationships:

1. A cross-sectional study provides some evidence as to possible causal relations among variables because it can establish an association among them.

2. A longitudinal study is superior because it not only identifies an association among variables but, additionally, it indicates the order of changes taking place in them.

3. A controlled experiment is still more superior in that it can establish a temporal sequence for the changes in variables but is also able to eliminate the effect of potentially confounding variables.

Although controlled experiments are the superior study design in isolating cause-effect relationships, they are relatively rare. Most of the body of knowledge assimilated by mankind has not been obtained through the use of controlled experiments but has come through informal observation of the associations and sequences of events around us, along with a large measure of trial and error.

Apparently the American Indians chewed willow bark as a medicine; it was later discovered to contain a natural form of aspirin. It is interesting to speculate about how they discovered this. From the beginning of time, mankind has probably tried every living plant in search of the miracle cure. They were not encouraged to chew poisonous plants, as they did not get better from them. Sorting out plants which had no medicinal effect from those which did was much more difficult since most people who are ill will get better because of the body's own curative powers.

The state of management knowledge is probably such that the disastrous approaches have been eliminated, but there is little assurance that the ineffectual ones have been distinguished from the effectual ones. If controlled experiments offer such power in isolating true causal relationships in business and elsewhere, why are they so relatively rare? There are two answers to this question. One answer is that the application of experimentation to business problems is relatively new. As a result, the sophistication of both researchers and managers is increasing.

The second reason why controlled experimentation in business is limited is that it is very difficult, and sometimes impossible, to implement. Controlled experimentation is relatively well developed in advertising research because the unit of study is often the individual consumer. It is relatively simple to study matched samples of individuals in controlled situations.

However, if the units of analysis are few and large, then such experimentation is quite difficult. The fact that economic policymakers must sort through a myriad of conflicting explanations for the same set of longitudinal data does not indicate the simplicity of economists. Rather, it indicates the complexity of economics. It would be impossible to conduct a controlled experiment with the U.S. economy—even if someone wanted to do so. There is no way that the discount rate could be changed while holding all other economic variables constant in order to determine its impact on housing starts.

Likewise, medical researchers cannot be labeled as unsophisticated because they evaluate the impact of smoking with the use of cross-sectional and longitudinal studies. Rather, these research designs are used because of the impossibility of taking a random sample of adolescents and dividing them into a group that smokes and another that does not (probably the most difficult part) and observing them as they grow into adulthood.

Where does this leave managers? First, they must work closely with researchers to identify where experimentation can be implemented cost-effectively. Second, managers themselves must be able to differentiate between controlled experiments and other forms of research before they bet corporate dollars on assumed cause-effect relationships. A healthy skepticism about rival explanations for technically accurate research results is important. The fact that all of the errors discussed in the previous chapters have been dealt with properly means little if the desire is to isolate cause-effect relations. The numerical findings for a cross-sectional study and an experimental study may be equally accurate, but only the latter offers any real hope that causal inferences can be made conclusively.

CHAPTER 6

How to Read the Research Report

Then there is the man who drowned crossing a stream with an average depth of six inches.

W. I. E. Gates

Statistics are like a bikini. What they reveal is suggestive, but what they conceal is vital.

Aaron Levenstein

Well-written research reports represent a reasonable compromise between presenting the results clearly and succinctly so that managers with little interest in the technical details can read them quickly, and presenting the methodology and analysis in sufficient detail that the foundation upon which the findings are based can be evaluated. Although the organization of research reports varies considerably in detail, they are generally arranged in the same manner as a newspaper article, with sections in order of descending general interest. Thus, a report may begin with a statement of the study's objectives and principal findings, continue with a more detailed description of the study and the data analysis, and conclude with supporting technical appendices, including such things as a copy of the questionnaire, a description of the sampling procedures, and the treatment of sampling error. Some research reports may even have a section pointing out the limitations of the study.

This chapter contains three sections. The first discusses the importance of reviewing the methodology section of the research report before accepting its findings and recommendations. The second discusses the way in which statistical data can be presented in a misleading fashion. The third presents a checklist of questions to be used by managers in evaluating business research projects.

• EXAMINING THE TECHNICAL DETAIL OF A RESEARCH REPORT

Several years ago a woman applied to a state public utilities commission for a license to offer mobile telephone service. As part of the application, an impressive looking document was submitted containing the results of a survey that had been conducted. Although the document contained virtually no detail concerning the study's methodology, it indicated that the respondents felt the existing services in the area were inadequate and that they were eager to receive those of the new carrier if the license were granted. Based on this study, the staff of the commission recommended prior to the hearing that the license should be granted.

During the hearing, the lawyer representing the firm that was protesting the application questioned the woman about the methodological detail left out of the report. It was found that the woman had designed the study herself and that the operators of the answering service she owned had conducted the interviews. A point was made of the fact that a conflict of interest was involved and that neither she nor her employees had any previous training or experience in doing research. Finally, it was discovered that no random sample was used but that the sample consisted only of existing customers of the answering service. In fact, some of these individuals and businesses were interviewed more than once for the study. After the hearing, the red-faced commission staff reversed its opinion that sufficient demand to support the license had been demonstrated.

The reason for including the technical detail in the

report itself, or at least making it available in a supporting document, is to allow the reader to examine two assumptions: (1) that the researchers chose and implemented reasonable research procedures, given the objectives of the study and existing contraints on money and time; and (2) that the conclusions of the study are logical extensions of these research procedures and the analyzed data which resulted from them. *The basic question is whether other competent researchers would tend to produce the same results and conclusions if they had been given the problem and resources provided the original researchers.*

A vast number of studies cannot withstand this test for one of several reasons. First, *many research reports simply do not contain enough detail to enable such an evaluation.* This is particularly true when the results are being made to the press or the general public. Unfortunately, this is an area where most of the abuses of research probably occur. I have seen politicians release survey results in which each candidate in a race has more than 50 percent of public support (a mathematical impossibility outside an election year). The reader can be assured that the biased questions presented in Chapter 3 were not included along with the press releases announcing what the public's beliefs were purported to be.

Unfortunately, most reporters do not have the background to make technical evaluations of research and rarely consult those who do. As a consequence, good and bad research are often undifferentiated in news reporting. In self defense, readers or viewers of reported research results should ask themselves if the sponsors of the research have a stake in the outcome. If they do, then it is important to determine whether the research was conducted by an established and independent research organization which invests in its professional integrity.

A second category of inadequate research reports is where *there is a great leap of faith or "expert opinion" from data to conclusions.* Many feasibility studies are of this sort. In a report for a new motel, for example, there may be a major gap between the detailed presentation of economic data for the area and the pro forma income statements and balance sheets that are included. The conclusions are based upon the subjective opinions of the researcher rather than on an economic or statistical model which translates the economic data into an estimate of the project's success or failure. Thus, the findings in any one of the tables of economic data can be changed without any obvious direct effect on the estimated outcome for the project. (It is interesting to speculate why reports recommending against projects in these feasibility studies are so rare.)

The weakness of these studies is often strikingly apparent when they are used to support the application for a license or charter in an industry regulated by state or federal government. Expert witnesses will use economic statistics or other forms of data to argue that the public good will be served by granting another bank charter, for example, while the expert witnesses of the protesting banks will use the same data to argue that there is hardly enough market to support a new bank.

Generally, economic or statistical models do exist, or can at least be constructed, to bridge the gap between economic data and forecasted results for a project. While these models may be simple and often involve questionable assumptions, an objective discussion of them is superior to comparing opposing expert witnesses on the basis of their grade point averages in graduate school.

A third category of problems is found where *an examination of the research report reveals major errors or limitations.* It is primarily for these situations that the previous chapters have been included to help the manager sort research projects into three categories: (1) those which are done sufficiently well that the findings can be accepted with little qualification; (2) those which suffer from some limitations or errors so that the results can be accepted with substantial modification or qualification; and (3) those which have such severe limitations that they should be rejected.

• EVALUATING THE PRESENTATION OF DATA

Because the study of statistics is so complex in itself, it is certainly impossible to prepare managers to evaluate the presentation of statistical data as it exists in its many and varied forms. Fortunately, the vast majority of research reports employ only the most elementary forms of statistical analysis, such as averages and percentages. A few cautionary points will be made about such analysis and the use of graphs.

The term *average* is often used rather loosely and can refer to any one of three common measures calculated by a statistician. The most common is the *mean,* or arithmetic average, which is calculated by adding a set of scores and dividing the sum by the number of scores in the set. For example, the mean family size in this country is approximately 3.3 members. A second measure is the *mode,* which is the most frequently occurring score in the set. Thus, the modal family size is 2, as more families have 2 members than any other number. The third measure is the *median,* which is calculated by ordering the scores from largest to smallest and picking the middle one. If all families were ordered according to size, and the family in the middle of the ordering would have 3 members, then that is the median.

If the distribution of scores is symmetrical, as would be the case if it resembled a bell-shaped (or normal) curve, the mean, mode, and median would be equal to each other. However, this is not the case if the distribution is asymmetrical. For example, the distribution of housing costs in this country is highly asymmetrical (statisticians would say positively skewed, but never in mixed company), because the vast majority of them cost less than $100,000 but some reach into the millions.

Since it is very sensitive to extreme values, the mean cost would be the highest, followed by the median, and the mode would be the lowest. A researcher wishing to exaggerate the expense of today's housing would report the mean, while one wishing to downplay it would report the mode. Government housing statistics tend to use the median because it gives a more balanced picture of housing costs.

Several points of caution should be made about the use of percentages. One is that *percentages can create an inflated picture of growth if the base is small.* A publisher was considering terminating a regional magazine because it had not gotten out of the red. In a presentation before the board, a member of the magazine's staff compared the ailing magazine's growth in sales with that of a highly successful national magazine by use of a graph similar to the one shown in Figure 6.1. What the staff member failed to point out was that any projected increase in sales would produce a large percentage increase simply because new subscribers were joining a very select group.

Caution should also be used in interpreting percentages as they are found in large tables. Figure 6.2 pres-

FIGURE 6.1

Percentage Growth of a National and a Regional Publication over the Last Three Years

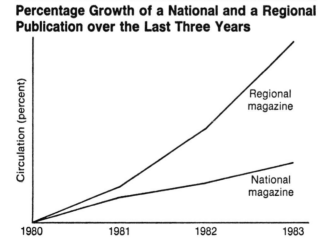

FIGURE 6.2

Correct Indication of the Percentage of Shopping Center Customers from Various Income Groups

Shopping Center

Income Level	Northgate	Eastgate	Westgate	Southgate	Centergate
Less than $10,000	37	12	16	31	21
$10,000–$19,999	26	32	37	42	26
$20,000–$29,999	22	38	41	15	28
$30,000–$39,999	10	15	4	9	21
$40,000 and over	5	3	2	3	4
Total	100	100	100	100	100

ents a study for a shopping mall and indicates the percentage of shoppers in various income classes that shop most frequently at various malls. The percentages correctly total 100 for each income class.

Figure 6.3 presents the same data but in a manner likely to be misinterpreted. The author actually saw a table similar to this where the researchers concluded that because the percentages for the highest income group did not add up to 100, it meant that these customers were shopping in a neighboring city. Actually, the percentages add to 100 for each shopping center and indicate what percentage of their customers are within each income group. Not surprisingly, the highest-income customers accounted for a small percentage of the customers for each shopping center, but this does

FIGURE 6.3

Incorrect Indication of the Percentage of Shopping Center Customers from Various Income Groups

Income Level

Shopping Center	Less than $10,000	$10,000–$19,999	$20,000–$29,999	$30,000–$39,999	Over $40,000
Northgate	37	26	22	10	5
Eastgate	12	32	38	15	3
Westgate	16	37	41	4	2
Southgate	31	42	15	9	3
Centergate	21	26	28	21	4

not mean that they leave town to shop. The table would have to be recalculated to indicate what percentage of each income group shops at the various shopping centers.

A word of caution should also be said about distorting meaning when using line charts. *By the selective choice of the origins and units of measurement for the horizontal and vertical axes, small rates of change can be made to look large and large ones can be made to look small.* Figures 6.4 and 6.5 both present the same data on the growth of advertising for a small newspaper. Notice that in Figure 6.4, the origin for dollars of advertising is $500,000 rather than zero, and the units of measurement for time are compressed as compared to

FIGURE 6.4

Projected Classified Advertising Revenue for *The Daily Gossip*

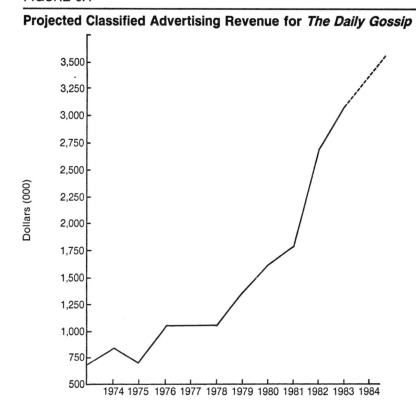

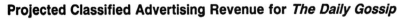

FIGURE 6.5

Projected Classified Advertising Revenue for *The Daily Gossip*

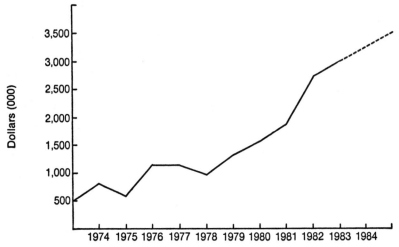

Figure 6.5. Thus, it creates the illusion of substantial growth.

Unfortunately, many of the data illusions just discussed appear in the popular and business presses, and the variety of these illusions is greater than presented here. For this reason it is important that managers:

1. Examine the details of a chart or graph before drawing any conclusion based upon an initial visual impression.

2. Use caution before accepting the presentation of averages and percentages at face value.

- ## QUESTIONS FOR EVALUATING A BUSINESS RESEARCH PROJECT

Chapter 2 discussed the problems that are encountered if the research is not relevant to the true problem. The responsibility for properly defining the problem rests with both the managers and the researchers and should have been addressed in the initial qualitative stage of the study. However, it is especially important for managers who have not been involved in the research process to ask:

1. Is the research based on a clear understanding of the problem it attempts to address?
2. Does the research include all of the significant variables which are relevant to the problem and are within the control of management?

Chapter 3 was concerned with measurement error which is one of the most difficult and intangible problems in business research. Problems of measurement error concern both the design and use of measurement instruments:

3. Does an examination of any questionnaire used suggest that there may be a problem of ambiguity when the interviewers communicate with the respondents and vice versa?
4. If researchers make inferences from the behavior of individuals rather than communicating with them directly, are there alternative explanations for that behavior?
5. Does an examination of any questionnaire used reveal editorializing or the use of inflamatory words which might bias responses to the questions asked?
6. If univariate, bivariate, or multivariate models are used to summarize data, are the assumptions of the model appropriate under the circumstances?
7. If questions are asked of respondents, are they ones the respondents are capable of answering?
8. Is there any reason to believe that respondents may be unwilling to answer questions candidly?
9. Are the interviewers sufficiently well trained and neutral on the research topic that they can be expected to obtain information from respondents accurately?

Chapter 4 discussed four types of error which limit the ability of researchers to generalize sample results to the populations from which the samples were selected. Accordingly, the following questions should be asked:

10. Does the frame adequately represent the target population for the study and minimize improper inclusions or exclusions? Are those improperly included or excluded likely to be different in a significant way from those properly included?

11. Is there a significant number of nonrespondents in the study who were either unwilling or unable to participate in the study? Are respondents likely to be different from nonrespondents in any meaningful way?

12. Was a probability sampling technique used, or is there a danger that some members of the frame have a disproportionately high probability of being selected while the probability is low for others? Is there any important difference between those sampled and those not?

13. Does the study demonstrate that the sample size was adequate to reduce sampling error to an acceptable minimum?

Chapter 5 is concerned with identifying cause-effect relationships and discusses the dangers of internal and external invalidity:

14. If causal inferences are made from a study, is there adequate experimental control to ensure that all rival explanations for a cause-effect relationship can be eliminated?

15. Is there any reason to believe that the causal inference which appears valid in the study under examination cannot be extended to another situation of interest?

If managers, armed with common sense and a modest degree of skepticism, can answer these questions to their satisfaction, then they can use the research findings with confidence. To the extent that unsatisfactory answers result, managers must work with researchers to qualify the findings by considering the nature and extent of the specific problem. However, if the problems are multiple and severe, then it may be wise to disregard the findings altogether.

• CONCLUSION

I feel some apprehension upon completing this book. A concern is that readers will have become so wary of research that they are tempted to avoid it altogether. It is sincerely hoped that this is not the case. The information gathered through research will never replace the experience and common sense of managers in making important business decisions, but it will buttress them, and as researchers and managers grow in sophistication, the possibility for reducing the risk surrounding major decisions will increase. (Besides, basing a decision on research will give managers someone else to blame if the decision turns sour.)

A related concern is that the references to abuses of research will encourage an adversarial relationship between managers and researchers. Most researchers have high professional standards and strive to provide the best information available to support managers' decisions. While problems do exist because of the unwillingness or inability of researchers, it is more often the case that researchers are falsely blamed. Research that confirms the opinions of managers is said to have been a waste of time and money, while research inconsistent with the opinions of managers is often dismissed as being in error. Researchers can empathize with portrait photographers who are often simply criticized as the bearers of bad news.

Rather than encourage an adversarial relationship between managers and researchers, it is hoped that this book will cause managers to have increased respect for researchers who work diligently to avoid the problems that have been discussed. Better communication between the two parties can only increase the effectiveness of each.

It is also my desire that this book serves to increase the reader's interest in the practice of research—both because it is important and because it can be fascinating. In this hope, an annotated bibliography has been provided.

ANNOTATED BIBLIOGRAPHY

Campbell, Stephen K. *Flaws and Fallacies in Statistical Thinking.* Englewood Cliffs, N.J.: Prentice-Hall, 1974.
 A small book similar to, but somewhat more substantial than, Darrell Huff's *How to Lie with Statistics.*

Converse, Jean M., and Howard Schuman. *Conversations at Random: Survey Research as Interviewers See It.* New York: John Wiley Sons, 1974.
 An entertaining and informative view of research from the perspective of those "in the trenches"—the field interviewers.

Cox, Eli P., III. *Marketing Research: Information for Decision Making.* New York: Harper Row, 1979.
 An elementary undergraduate marketing research textbook. It takes a relatively nontechnical perspective predicated on the realization that the vast majority of marketing students will be research users rather than researchers. Although it is limited in its coverage of the other problem areas of business, it would probably serve as a reasonable supplementary text to *Evaluating Complex Business Reports: A Guide for Executives.*

Churchill, Gilbert A., Jr. *Marketing Research: Methodological Foundations.* 3d ed. Hinsdale, Ill.: Dryden Press, 1983.

An advanced undergraduate or graduate marketing research textbook. It has a relatively technical emphasis with a thorough discussion of statistical analysis.

Dillman, Don A. *Mail and Telephone Surveys: The Total Design Method.* New York: John Wiley Sons, 1978.

A thorough discussion of mail and telephone survey methods, which have replaced personal interviews as the dominant medium.

Dunham, Randall B., and Frank J. Smith. *Organizational Surveys: an Internal Assessment of Organizational Health.* Glenview, Ill.: Scott, Foresman, 1979.

A brief, applications-oriented discussion of a specialized application of survey research.

Erdos, Paul L. *Professional Mail Surveys.* New York: McGraw-Hill, 1970.

A detailed, applications-oriented discussion of mail surveys by one of their earliest proponents.

Ferber, Robert, ed. *Handbook of Marketing Research.* New York: McGraw-Hill, 1974.

A large collection of articles written by academics and professional researchers on a wide variety of topics. It is written for the researcher but can be helpful to the research user who is interested in obtaining more detail on selected research topics. Unfortunately, no such book exists for business research in general.

Ferber, Robert; Alain Cousineau; Millard Crask; and Hugh G. Wales, eds. *A Basic Bibliography on Marketing Research.* Chicago: American Marketing Association, 1974.

An excellent, if somewhat outdated, bibliography of technical articles on marketing research.

Gould, Stephen J. *The Mismeasure of Man.* New York: W. W. Norton, 1983.

A fascinating history of the measurement of intelligence. It reveals how "scientific" research has been abused to confirm and protect society's worst prejudices. Although the book has little to do with business research, it does encourage a healthy mistrust of scientists and has something to offend everyone but the most insensitive, healthy, white males of northern European descent.

Green, Paul E., and Donald S. Tull. *Research for Marketing Decisions.* 3d ed. Englewood Cliffs, N.J.: Prentice-Hall, 1975.
A graduate marketing research textbook. It has a technical emphasis and has a particularly good discussion of multivariate statistical techniques, such as multiple regression.

Groves, Robert M., and Robert L. Khan. *Surveys by Telephone: A National Comparison with Personal Interviews.* New York: Academic Press, 1979.
The report of the results of an extensive comparison of the two interviewing media. The conclusion is essentially that the additional costs of personal interviews can be justified by their superior results.

Huff, Darrell. *How to Lie with Statistics.* New York: W. W. Norton, 1954.
This book is a wonderful little piece to support the claim that there are "lies, damn lies, and statistics." It provides many illustrations of the ways in which statistics and their presentation can be used to distort information rather than to reveal it.

Labaw, Patricia. *Advanced Questionnaire Design.* Cambridge, Mass.: Abt Books, 1980.
The title is somewhat misleading for this short, rather nontechnical discussion of questionnaire design. It is a good complement to the text by Sudman and Bradburn.

Moroney, M. J. *Facts from Figures.* Baltimore: Penguin Books, 1961.
An excellent and rather technical book similar to those of Huff and Campbell.

Payne, Stanley S. *The Art of Asking Questions.* Princeton, N.J.: Princeton University Press, 1951.
A wonderful, small, and nontechnical classic on question wording. It is a useful book and fun to read.

Sudman, Seymour. *Applied Sampling.* New York: Academic Press, 1976.

A brief, technical discussion of the most common sampling procedures and their use. Although the book is probably used more by researchers than research users, it is appealing in that it is less esoteric and more user-friendly than most of the books on sampling.

Sudman, Seymour, and Norman M. Bradburn. *Asking Questions: A Practical Guide to Questionnaire Design*. San Francisco: Jossey-Bass Publishers, 1983.

A book dedicated to Stanley Payne who wrote *The Art of Asking Questions*. This book is an up-to-date and comprehensive treatment of questionnaire design.

Tull, Donald S., and Gerald S. Albaum. *Survey Research: A Decisional Approach*. New York: Intext Educational Publishers, 1973.

A brief but somewhat technical discussion of the methodology of survey rescarch, applicable primarily to cross-sectional studies.

INDEX